Alone At Home

The *Emerson Moore* Adventures by Bob Adamov

- *Rainbow's End* — Released October 2002
- *Pierce the Veil* — Released May 2004
- *When Rainbows Walk* — Released June 2005
- *Promised Land* — Released July 2006
- *The Other Side of Hell* — Released June 2008
- *Tan Lines* — Released June 2010
- *Sandustee* — Released March 2013
- *Zenobia* — Released May 2014
- *Missing* — Released April 2015
- *Golden Torpedo* — Released July 2017
- *Chincoteague Calm* — Released April 2018
- *Flight* — Released May 2019
- *Assateague Dark* — Released May 2020
- *Sunset Blues* — Released May 2022
- *White Spider Night* — Released July 2022
- *Rainbow's End 20th Anniversary Edition* — Released October 2022
- *Sawdust Joint* — Released July 2023
- *Holden's Promise* — Released March 2024

The *Zeke Layne* Adventure by Bob Adamov

Memory Layne — Released May 2021

Next *Emerson Moore* Adventure:
Breakwater Bay

Alone At Home

Bob Adamov

Packard Island Publishing

Wooster, Ohio

2024

www.packardislandpublishing.com

www.BobAdamov.com

This book is a work of fiction. Names, characters, places and incidents are either products of the author's imagination or are used fictitiously. Any resemblance to actual events, locales or persons, living or dead, is entirely coincidental.

First edition • September 2024

ISBN: 979-8-9853593-6-7

Printed and bound in the United States of America

Cover Art/Layout by: Ryan Sigler
Blue River Digital
303 Towerview Dr.
Columbia City, IN 46725
www.blueriverd.com

Published by:
Packard Island Publishing
3025 Evergreen Drive
Wooster, OH 44691
packardislandpublishing.com

Praise, Reviews and Awards for Bob Adamov's Novels

"… Adamov is a superb craftsman of hanging-on-the-edge-of-your-seat mystery adventures…"– Midwest Book Review

"… Adamov's natural flair for originality and a narrative storytelling style that is laced with unexpected plot twists and turns that will keep and hold the reader's fully entertained and rapt attention from cover to cover!" – Midwest Book Review

Adamov Voted **2022 Best Lake Erie Author** – Lake Erie Living magazine

"One of **PublishOhio's Favorite Authors***"* – PublishOhio.com

"Memory Layne Named **Best Fiction Novel** *and* **Action Adventure Finalist***"* – 2022 Next Generation Indie Awards

*"***A Great Read!***"* – Clive Cussler

"…Enough action to satiate James Bond fans…" – Lansing State Journal

"Memory Layne reminds me of Nicholas Sparks' The Notebook!" – Charles Meier, Key West author and star of the Science Channel's The Curse of The Bermuda Triangle

" **Great Local Book!***"* – Eastern Shore of Virginia Tourism

"This book is like slipping on a pair of broken-in boat moccasins – comfortable and familiar." – Cleveland Magazine

*"***Honorable Mention***"* – Great Midwest, Florida, Hollywood, New York & London Book Festivals

"One of the best novels in northeast Ohio!" – Akron Beacon Journal

"…Fascinating tale of corporate greed, violence, and betrayal …" – Sun Newspapers

"This series is a must read for any diver or Clive Cussler fan! – Visibility Divers' Magazine

*"***2003 Great Lakes Book Award Finalist***"* – Great Lakes Independent Booksellers Association

Dedication

This book is a tribute to Jack and Phyllis Bishop, two friends who have been a part of my life since 1969. Our friendship began in the days of Goodyear, where Jack and I were colleagues. I was a fan of Jack's band, always in the audience during their performances. It's been a joy to immortalize them as characters in this narrative, showcasing their vibrant and compassionate spirits. Their essence is woven into the fabric of this story, a testament to the enduring bond we share and the fact that I named my daughter Jill after their daughter, Jill Tracy.

This book is also dedicated to Bill Vail, my inspirational English teacher from Norton High School, who introduced me to a world inhabited by literary titans such as Emerson and Thoreau. Bill encouraged me to venture beyond my comfort zone, guiding me through the art of humorous interpretation within the National Forensic League, which was instrumental in conquering my reluctance to speak publicly. His influence has been profoundly positive, touching the lives of countless students.

This book is affectionately dedicated to Pastor Nick Cleveland of Wooster Grace Church, whose humility and servant leadership shine with a Christlike glow. It's always in good fun that I rib him about his amusing aversion to felines. It seems only fitting that such a book should honor him.

They that wait upon the Lord shall renew their strength;
they shall mount up with wings as eagles;
they shall run, and not be weary;
and they shall walk, and not faint.
— Isaiah 40:31

Acknowledgments

I'd like to thank my amazing senior editor John Wisse and my team of editors: Cathy Adamov and Michelle Marchese for their efforts in improving my creative works. They all do a tremendous job in supporting me.

I'd also like to acknowledge the inspiration that my own eight-year-old grandson Hudson (aka "Little Grandpa") gave me in writing this book and creating a character somewhat based on his antics.

I'd be in trouble if I didn't acknowledge my other grandchildren – Alexandra, Graham, Brooks and Harper for also inspiring me.

For My Readers

Have fun trying to determine which of the incidents in this novel actually happened to me due to my clumsiness or inattention. Also, FYI, I happen to love cats although I have been known to occasionally step on their tails.

Alone At Home

CHAPTER 1

Monday Morning

Nestled along the coastline, where the Cape Fear River greets the vast Atlantic Ocean, lies the idyllic and historic waterfront town of Southport, North Carolina. The charming facades of its historic homes are a blend of Victorian, Cape Cod, and colonial styles featuring wide porches with rocking chairs that seemingly lure passersby to sit.

Its streets, each lined by a canopy of live oaks, are caressed by the soft whispers of the ocean breeze and dappled by sunlight filtering through the Spanish moss-draped branches.

In the East Moore Street driveway of a cozy, sun-kissed yellow cottage, under one of these ancient trees, sat a car. It was eagerly waiting to be filled with a couple of suitcases, in preparation for a trip five days before Christmas.

"Honey, can you put my suitcases in the car?" the 72-year-old, gray-haired Charlotte Ivers asked her husband, George.

"Where are they?" the cantankerous Ivers grumbled. The 80-year-old, balding curmudgeon wasn't excited about his wife leaving him home alone for nearly a week while she visited her sister in Raleigh. Her sister was recovering from surgery and needed someone to be with her for a short period.

"George, I put them next to the front door," she called from the front bedroom.

The white-bearded Ivers walked through the one-story house to the front door where he spied two bulging suitcases. Carefully, the lanky octogenarian lifted them. They were heavy.

"What all do you have in here? You're going to give me a hernia," he grimaced as he lugged them through the doorway to the car.

"I threw in a couple of gifts for my sister. Here, I'll pop the trunk for you," she called as she walked onto the front porch. She depressed her key fob, and the car doors and trunk lid unlocked. "Why aren't you using your cane?" she asked as she noticed the cane leaning against the porch railing.

Ivers turned to face her. Raising the straw hat that covered his balding head, he remarked, "I don't need it. My sciatic nerve is doing better. I can walk without it."

Charlotte's face filled with skepticism. "I don't want you falling down and getting hurt."

"I won't," he reassured her. He didn't like the cane. It was a sign of weakness in his mind. "But I'll save it in case I become a carnival barker," he growled.

Turning his attention back to the car, Ivers raised the trunk lid as his cellphone buzzed. He looked at the phone and saw it was his insurance agent in nearby Wilmington.

"Charlie. Let me call you back in a few," Ivers answered. "Charlotte is getting ready to leave for Raleigh to visit her sister."

"Okay. I'll stand by."

Ivers ended the call and set his cellphone on the trunk floor. Taking both hands, he heaved the first suitcase into the trunk, then the second.

"Oh my," he grunted as he stepped back from the vehicle.

"Oh George, are you all right?" his wife asked as she neared him.

Ivers leaned against the car. He took several deep breaths as Charlotte watched him closely. She knew that he could be a real drama king at times, exaggerating his aches and pains. At other times though, she had a growing concern about his clumsiness and forgetfulness.

"I'll be fine. Just let me catch my breath," he groused.

Charlotte set a large red bag on the white limestone driveway.

"Could you put my makeup bag in the back seat for me? I forgot my Bible. I left it inside," she said as she turned and walked briskly back inside the bungalow framed by two live oak trees in its neatly landscaped yard.

"Yeah. I guess I can," Ivers mumbled as he picked it up and walked around the car. He opened the door behind the driver's seat and placed the makeup bag inside. As he closed the door, she reappeared, closing the trunk lid while she walked around the car.

She opened the driver's door, then turned to Ivers. "George, I want you to be sure to take care of my cat."

Ivers grimaced. He didn't like the cat. He was hoping that it would run off. "Why can't we get rid of your cat?"

"George! How could you say that let alone think that way? You know how precious Snookums is to me," she countered defiantly.

She picked up the cat and stroked its gray fur. "Momma's going to miss you," she said with a voice laced with sadness. She kissed the cat on top of its head and scratched behind its ears several times before placing it on the driveway. "I'll be back Christmas Eve, and I promise to bring you something special," she said lovingly.

Ivers frowned as he watched the two. "When you return, I've decided to buy you a new pair of eyeglasses," Ivers suggested.

"Whatever for? These aren't six months old," she asked with a quizzical look as one hand went to touch the eyeglass frame on her face.

"I thought they'd help you see things my way," he said half-seriously.

"George!" she fumed quietly before continuing. "It would be a good time for you and Snookums to become good friends."

Ivers looked down at the furry, gray cat who was sitting on the driveway, watching the exchange. The cat looked up at Ivers who swore that the cat gave him a death stare. It then walked over to his wife to rub up against her calf and purr one last time before she left.

"Little Snookums, I wish I could take you with me, but Daddy will take care of you," Charlotte cooed as she picked up the cat again and stroked it.

Yep, right to the Humane Society drop-off, Ivers thought quietly.

"You will take care of little Snookums, won't you dear?" she asked as she placed the cat on the ground.

"Yes. Of course," Ivers spoke with disdain through clenched teeth. The green-eyed feline merely blinked slowly while its tail gave a solitary, graceful twitch.

Charlotte leaned toward Ivers as she puckered her lips. "Give me a kiss goodbye, George."

Ivers looked up and down the street. "Out here? In public?" he asked with consternation.

"Who cares?" she asked as she quickly moved in and gave him a quick peck on his lips.

Stepping back, Ivers used the back of his hand to wipe his lips. "You probably got that red lipstick all over me. What are the neighbors going to think if they see me with red lipstick on my lips?" Ivers fussed.

"Maybe you're loosening up? And who is going to get that

close to you anyway? You always do your best to get lost any time a neighbor drops by," she countered.

Ivers grumbled softly to himself.

"And be sure to change Snookum's litter box," she called as she stepped into the car.

Ivers frowned at having to change the litter box, something he never did. Ivers shut his wife's car door and returned to the porch. He picked up the cane and held it in his right hand while he doffed his straw hat to say goodbye to his wife. Blissfully unaware that the cat had joined him on the porch, he took a step sideways, stepping on its plush tail.

Screeching loudly as a banshee as Ivers jumped back in surprise, the cat ran up a nearby tree. From its elevated safety, the cat glared down at Ivers with slit-like eyes filled with displeasure.

"Did you do that on purpose? Hurt my little Snookums?" Charlotte asked with narrowed eyes as she looked out of the open window, concerned for her beloved pet. Her glare was both accusatory and forgiving while reflecting her frustration with her husband's well-known aversion to cats.

"No dear," he answered quickly. But when I do, you won't know, he thought with evil glee. "And don't stop at any yard sales on your trip," he cautioned his wife who had a penchant for buying knick-knacks from those sales. He wanted to change her name to Yard Sale Charlotte, the woman who never saw a yard sale that she could drive past.

"That wasn't part of my plan," she countered with mock consternation.

It didn't have to be, Ivers thought.

"If you need anything from the store, you can ask the Bishops to give you a ride there," Charlotte suggested.

The Bishops, who were in their early sixties, lived next door. Phyllis was Charlotte's closest friend. It seemed like they visited each other almost every day. Phyllis' husband was Jack, a goateed guitar player who could be heard halfway to Wilmington when he practiced on his electric guitar, often awakening Ivers from his afternoon naps. At other times, Ivers would hear Jack singing. He sounded like a dying whale.

Charlotte continued with her instructions. "And change out of that flannel shirt. It's going to be a warm day today. And wear your eyeglasses. I don't want you to trip over something. You know how clumsy you can be," she droned.

"Yes, dear," he acknowledged begrudgingly.

Charlotte started the car. "Oh, one more thing, George."

"What's that?" he asked, wondering if she was ever going to drive away.

"You can put up the Christmas tree while I'm gone. I've been so busy that I didn't have a chance to set it up." Then she added, "The garland and wreath look nice on the porch even though I had to put those up myself."

Ivers frowned. He didn't like all of the decorating for Christmas. "I don't know where the tree or the other decorations are," he fretted, while hoping that she would say that he could forget it. That didn't work.

"They're in the basement on the top shelf. If you can't get them, ask one of the neighbors to help. See you Christmas Eve!" she called.

That visiting his neighbors stuff was another thing that wasn't going to happen. Ivers liked minding his own business. He wasn't the social butterfly like his wife.

"Did you hear me, George?" she shouted as she put the car in gear, and it started moving down the driveway.

"Yeah. Yeah," Ivers answered as he moved the small wood block that kept the door from shutting and locking him out. He had been procrastinating about fixing that front door lock. With regard to the Christmas tree, he had no intention of following through with her request. He was going to enjoy his time alone at home, and he already had his first task in mind.

Ivers glanced at the cat as it climbed down the tree. "Come on Snookums. I'll give you a treat," Ivers called slyly while his wife drove away.

The cat understood the word "treat" and scurried across the yard to the door which Ivers quickly shut. As the cat tried to brake, it slammed into the closed door.

"Heh, heh," he laughed wickedly as he reopened the door and teased the spoiled cat. Next, Ivers placed his cane next to the sofa in the front living room before he walked to each of the two bathrooms. There, he raised the toilet seats. "Man-style", he grinned silently. He was going to enjoy nearly a week of not hearing "put the toilet seat down."

Ivers walked into the small living room that faced the street. He plopped into his easy chair and tilted it back. Before reaching for the TV remote, he placed his eyeglasses on his face and flicked on the TV. He was greeted by a picture of zig-zags that looked like a disco for digital ants. He then heard a gurgling noise as if the TV had just gargled with saltwater. Darn TV gremlins at work, Ivers thought with frustration.

The puzzled look on his face competed with the full frown on his mouth as he played with buttons on the remote. No matter what he did, he could not get a picture on the TV screen.

The look on his face was replaced by one of realization. He stood from his chair and walked to the front window. He stared at the spot near the fence line where he had been digging earlier that morning. He now remembered that area was where the internet/TV cable was buried. Gritting his teeth as he realized that he probably cut the cable, he decided to call the cable company to have them come out and repair it. He wasn't going to go any days with no TV.

Ivers reached into his pants pocket for his cellphone, but it wasn't there. He looked back at the end table next to his easy chair but didn't see it. He wandered into the kitchen and looked on the countertops, but no cellphone.

A thought struck him. He had set his cellphone in Charlotte's trunk when he had placed her suitcases inside. His cellphone was on its way to Raleigh with her. A large frown appeared on his face.

Dealing with the reality of the situation, Ivers decided to make lunch. He entered the kitchen and opened the refrigerator door. He saw the prepared food that his wife had made for him and removed the containers. Placing them on the counter, he read the labels: pea and broad bean couscous, beetroot and lentil salad, smashed avocado and wilted spinach, avocados with tuna, and Thai turkey meatballs in coconut curry.

Gathering the containers in his hands, he carried them to the kitchen trash can and dumped them. He wasn't going to eat any of that healthy stuff while she was gone. He was on his own meal plan, he grinned.

He returned to the fridge and found some sliced cheese, then decided to make two grilled cheese sandwiches for lunch. Ten minutes later, he set the hot sandwiches on the table and sat down. He couldn't wait to indulge in the simple pleasure of two piping hot grilled cheese sandwiches. The golden-brown toast and the cheese had melted to just the right degree of gooeyness, a small slice of heaven.

As he raised one of the delectable sandwiches to his mouth to take that first blissful bite, the doorbell rang. With a furrowed brow, his head snapped in the direction of the doorway. The bell rang again. Reluctantly, Ivers returned the sandwich to his plate and walked out of the kitchen, fussing to himself the entire way to the front door. Opening it, he was greeted by a cheery voice. It was Phyllis Bishop from next door.

"Hello George. I've got Charlotte on the phone. She said you left your cellphone in the car and she has it with her," the vivacious Phyllis said cheerfully as she fought to hold back a grin. "She wants to talk to you," Phyllis offered, handing her phone to Ivers.

"Thanks," he muttered. "You have my phone, huh?"

"Yes, dear. You left it in the trunk. I tried to call you and I heard it ringing back there. I pulled over and found it. I'll bring it home at the end of the week. If you need anything, Phyllis said you can come on over to her house to use her phone," Charlotte stated matter-of-factly.

"Okay."

"Did you have lunch yet?"

"Yes."

"Which container did you try?" she asked eagerly.

Ivers tried to recall the names on the containers. "I believe it was the chicken thigh meatballs," he stammered, trying to recall the name of one of the items that he had trashed.

"You mean the Thai turkey meatballs? I didn't make chicken thighs," she suggested.

"That was probably what it was. I can't remember," he fumbled.

"Well, you be careful. I'm driving into some traffic and better focus," she said as she ended the call.

As Ivers handed the cellphone back to Phyllis, he heard a voice pipe up from behind her.

"Mr. Ivers? Knock, knock."

A bewildered look filled Ivers' face as he peered around Phyllis to see a young boy looking up at him. The dark-haired boy's face was filled with a large smile. Two deep brown eyes beamed up at him from under a head full of shaggy brown hair.

"Oh my. I forgot to introduce you to my grandson. He's staying with us this week. This is Hudson. He's eight-years-old. Hudson, say hello to Mr. Ivers."

Ivers spoke first. "Looks more like a shaggy dog to me," he grimaced.

The boy popped out from behind his grandmother. "Hi Mr. Ivers. Knock, knock. I love knock-knock jokes. Don't you love them, too?" The words fired out of the highly-energized youth like machine gun bullets.

Wrinkling his brow, Ivers replied. "I don't like them, Hudson."

"Oh, try one. Try one, please." The boy was persistent.

"Okay," Ivers winced.

"Great. You start. Say knock, knock."

"Knock, knock," Ivers stated.

"Who's there?" Hudson grinned.

A confused look crossed Ivers' face. "I don't know. You're the one who wanted to play this game," he grumbled.

Hudson bent over laughing. Between giggles, he replied, "That's the joke. I'm the one who is supposed to say knock, knock, not you."

Ivers glared at the boy. He hoped the boy wasn't going to turn into a pest. Ivers lifted his eyes to Phyllis. "Thank you for coming over with your cellphone. I need to finish my lunch."

"No problem, George. I'm glad to help. Remember that we are here if you need anything," Phyllis offered graciously. She had been concerned for Ivers for the last several years when he went through a dramatic change in his approach to life. His once jovial manner had done a complete turnabout.

Ivers was already closing the front door as Hudson began, "I've got another one for you, Mr. Ivers. Knock, knock."

The door shut in the youngster's face, and Ivers made sure to lock it. He could hear the grandson talking as they walked away.

"That man's head is shaped like a big egg, Grandma."

Frowning, Ivers headed back to the kitchen as he thought about what his wife had said about Phyllis. She thought Phyllis was telepathic, that Phyllis sensed when his wife needed something. Ivers had countered that she was telecatholic because she could spread news faster than the pope.

He entered the kitchen and sat down at the table. He picked up his grilled cheese sandwich and bit into it. No surprise. It was cold as the cheese had congealed into a rubbery disappointment. He chewed silently as he looked absent-mindedly out the patio door to the fenced-in back yard.

Finished with his cold sandwiches, he picked off the crumbs from his majestic beard as a look of sheer frustration crossed his face. This was not how he envisioned his lunchtime escapade.

He then remembered that he didn't have cable TV or internet access. He should have asked Phyllis if he could use her phone to call the cable company to report the service interruption. He thought briefly about going next door to ask her but dismissed the rogue idea. He didn't like asking anyone for anything.

CHAPTER 2

Monday Afternoon

As Ivers stared out the patio door, he realized that it was an unusually warm December afternoon in Southport. It was 77°F and a perfect time to catch some sun with no interruptions.

Ivers carefully walked into the attached garage and switched on the overhead light. He then rummaged around the dark, cobwebbed corners where he thought he had last seen the pool. His heart skipped a beat when his hand brushed against something vinyl. With a big grin, he pulled out the two-foot-deep inflatable swimming pool, which hadn't been inflated in years.

He closely examined the deflated mass complete with patches from the last decade's puncture wounds. He remembered how he hated patching it but had bent to the task because he wasn't going to spend any money for a new pool. He then carried it outside, spread it across the patio and used an air pump to inflate it. Ivers turned on the outside faucet and dropped the end of the garden hose into the pool.

After returning the pump to the garage, he wandered inside the house to the master bedroom in the front of the house. Rummaging through his dresser drawer, he found his pair of pink swimming trunks. After slipping into them, he studied his aging body in the full-length mirror. His belly sagged and his chest drooped. He sucked in his gut as much as he could, then let it go with a rush of air. He had long lost that muscular physique years ago. He was no longer his wife's eye candy, he thought.

Nowadays, he found himself becoming more limited. His knees clicked and hurt, making him go down and up steps one at a time. He couldn't walk the beach anymore. The uneven sand made his hips ache.

The only ailment that had improved was his back pain – and that was due to the inexpensive mattress a friend of his wife's had suggested he order from Amazon. He clearly remembered fussing as it unrolled and slowly expanded to its ten-inch height. It was one of the rare, good pieces of advice he had received from a friend of his wife.

He stepped away from the mirror and walked back to the patio where he saw the pool was nearly filled. He shut off the faucet. When he turned back toward the pool, he saw a seagull swimming in it. That was one of the problems with living so close to the ocean and the Cape Fear River as there was always an abundance of seagulls.

Grabbing a nearby rake, he swung at the seagull which flapped its wings with a loud squawk and flew up before the rake could connect with it. Ivers swung again, but the seagull dodged the rake easily. It seemed like the seagull enjoyed taunting Ivers with its cries as he swung again, and again, and again, but he could not hit the seagull. It was just too fast and too smart for him.

Ivers spotted Snookums sitting on a patio chair. It seemed to be enjoying the old man's battle with the white-feathered, yellow-beaked seagull. Ivers swore that the cat was snickering at him.

"Snookums, why don't you get that seagull?" Ivers snapped angrily. "Stupid cat! I'll knock you into next week looking both ways for Sunday," he growled.

Then Ivers had an idea. He walked into the house and grabbed the container of cat treats from the counter. When he returned poolside, he placed several of the cat treats on the edge of the pool.

"You want a treat?" Ivers cooed unconvincingly as he stared at the cat. "Go get the birdie."

Snookums licked its lips and crouched low. It looked ready to pounce, but the cat was just playing with Ivers. It had been laughing silently as it watched Ivers' frustrated battle with the seagull. Ivers smiled at his ingenuity and turned back to look at the pool. The smile quickly disappeared as he saw the seagull pecking away at the cat treats.

"Get out of here!" Ivers yelled as he ran toward the seagull.

The seagull flapped its wings and flew up in the air, leaving behind a trail of droppings on the edge of the pool and the patio. Ivers was left baffled and frustrated, glaring at the seagull soaring overhead as it watched Ivers.

A revenge-filled Ivers decided to trick the seagull. He casually turned his back as he gripped the rake tightly. Out of the corner of his eyes, he saw the seagull land on the edge of the pool. Suddenly, Ivers whipped around and struck forcibly at the seagull. He missed it as it flapped upward, and the prongs of the rake sunk into the inflatable ring of the pool.

When Ivers pulled up the rake, he was greeted by the sound of hissing air, escaping from the holes that he had punctured. He also noticed the holes in the pool from the seagull pecking at the cat treats. With a series of victorious squawks, the seagull flew away. A frowning Ivers was left to stare at his deflating pool as water began to cascade across the patio.

Ivers soon finished emptying the remaining water from the pool and disposing it into the trash bin next to the one-car garage. He returned to the patio and scanned his backyard. It had a six-foot tall privacy fence around it, and there was a small storage shed near the rear corner of the yard. A live oak towered over it.

Still wanting to enjoy the unusually warm December afternoon, Ivers decided to catch some rays in the used zero-gravity chair that his wife previously had purchased at a garage sale. He pulled it out and set it in the sunlight near the edge of the patio.

He next returned inside the kitchen where he poured himself a glass of sweet tea. Taking the beverage outdoors, he came up with another idea. He was going to sun himself in the buff and surprise his wife with an all-over tan. He looked around to double-check that where he had positioned the chair didn't allow any of the neighbors to see him. Satisfied, he dropped his swimming trunks and sat in the chair.

Easing the chair back, he reached for his sweet tea and took a sip. After returning the tea to the table, he closed his eyes and relaxed under the sun's warm rays. The chair felt comfortable and cozy.

A few minutes later, Ivers shifted his weight. His movement was followed by the sound of a loud crack as his feet were elevated straight up and his head banged on the patio floor. The metal frame had broken, and Ivers felt a piece of metal jabbing into his side. He wondered if he had injured himself.

He tried to return the chair to its upright position, but it was broken beyond repair. He was stuck upside down and naked as he wondered how he was going to escape from his predicament. He was trapped in a whirlwind of nausea and panic. That's when he heard something he didn't want to hear.

"Mr. Ivers? Are you in the backyard?" Hudson called as the gate next to the garage squeaked open. "I knocked on your front door, but nobody answered. Hello?"

A panicked Ivers looked around for something to cover himself with. He saw his beach towel next to the glass of sweet tea and stretched to grab it. Quickly covering himself, he saw a wide-eyed Hudson walk around the corner of the garage.

"Mr. Ivers, what happened?" he asked with youthful bewilderment as his eyes went from the barely-covered old man to the swimming trunks on the patio floor.

"What happened Mr. Ivers?"

"My chair broke."

"I can help you. Are those your swimming trunks?"

"Yes. They fell off when the chair flipped back," Ivers explained unconvincingly.

Hudson walked over to the trunks. "That's really weird. I didn't know they could fly off like that."

"It's called environmental dynamics," Ivers offered hurriedly as he made up an excuse.

Hudson's forehead wrinkled as he tried to repeat Ivers' explanation. "Emental dinosaurs?"

"No Hudson. It's called environmental dynamics," Ivers explained.

"Okay. I get it." Hudson nodded, pretending to understand the profound wisdom being imparted. "How does that work?"

"Never mind. Just help me get up."

"How do I do that?"

Ivers assessed his situation. The chair was in a locked position. "Help me tip the chair over, but keep your eyes closed. Understand?"

"Oh yes. I'll keep my eyes closed," Hudson said quickly as he grabbed the side of the chair with his eyes shut. With Ivers throwing his weight and Hudson pulling on the side of the chair, they were able to tip it over.

Ivers rolled onto his side and grabbed his swimming trunks. He quickly pulled them on. "You can open your eyes, Hudson."

Carefully opening one eye, Hudson peeked to be sure that

Ivers had his trunks on. Satisfied, he opened both eyes. "Lucky it was me who came over here and not my grandmother."

Ivers nodded his head. He was anxious to go inside the house and get fully dressed. "Why did you come over, Hudson?"

"I have a new knock-knock joke for you. Do you want to hear it?"

Ivers didn't, but it was the least that he could do to humor the boy for rescuing him. "Go ahead."

"Knock, knock."

"Who's there?" Ivers sighed.

"Yoda lady."

"Yoda lady who?"

"I didn't know you could yodel," Hudson laughed.

"Ha-ha," Ivers groused.

"Guess what Mr. Ivers?"

"What?" Ivers was anxious for the overbearing youngster to leave.

"Grandpa Jack bought me a drum set. I get to play the drums when he practices on his guitar!" Hudson beamed.

Ivers groaned as he thought about the awful drum banging that soon would fill the air with noise.

"I better get back to grandma's house. I've got to tell her how I rescued you and how the mental dinosaurs made your trunks fall off," Hudson said proudly as he walked around the corner of the garage.

Ivers began to ask him not to say anything, but he felt it would be futile. Out of the corner of his eye, he saw Snookums. She hadn't budged and seemed to be enjoying Ivers' dilemma. Stupid cat, he thought as he walked into the house to change out of his swimming trunks.

An hour later, Ivers' rumbling stomach signaled dinner time.

He wandered into the kitchen and opened the fridge. Since he had thrown out the healthy meals his wife had prepared, the fridge didn't offer much. No problem, he thought as he shut the fridge door. He'd order pizza. He reached in his pocket for his cellphone, then remembered he had left it in his wife's car. No pizza tonight.

Reopening the fridge, he scanned it carefully. A smile crossed his face when he spotted a jar of strawberry jam. He placed the jam on the counter and grabbed a jar of peanut butter from the cupboard. Opening up the loaf of 16-grain wheat bread, he made himself two peanut butter and jelly sandwiches.

After devouring them, he washed them down with a glass of sweet tea. Tomorrow, he decided, he would make a visit to the convenience store, which was four blocks away, and load up on some goodies.

Placing his dish in the sink, he spotted a note on the counter. He picked it up. It was a reminder from his wife to take two tablespoons of his laxative daily. She was so concerned about him being constipated. He stared at the bottle on the counter when a noise at the patio door distracted him.

It was Snookums. The cat wanted inside and was climbing up the screen patio door. Ivers smiled as he realized how he could take revenge on the cat for not helping him with scaring away the seagull.

"Just a minute, Snookums," Ivers called with an evil glint in his eyes. He withdrew a can of salmon-flavored cat food from the cupboard and opened it. Next, he stirred in two tablespoons of his laxative.

Chuckling as he carried the opened can to the patio door, he slid the door open and walked outside. In the golden haze of an early evening, he leaned forward, the can of cat food in his hand, its contents glistening like culinary treasure and set it on the patio floor. The cat eyed the can with a predator's focus.

"Here's a tasty treat for you, Snookums," Ivers said as he quickly shut the door and stepped back. He couldn't help but chuckle, a gruff sound that rumbled from deep within. The cat had a bewildered look on its face as it was used to eating inside. The scent of salmon enticed its attention, and it began inhaling the cat food.

Meanwhile, Ivers had settled on a patio chair where he could watch the cat under the sun's waning rays. This would be his evening entertainment as he enjoyed the air, filled with the rich, briny scent of the sea.

Forty-five minutes passed, and there was no sign of any reaction from the cat. Maybe the laxative didn't have the same effect on cats. Ivers was bored with waiting and walked to the patio door. He opened to see what the cat would do as it usually raced inside any chance it had.

Instead of going inside, the cat just stared at him. Ivers swore silently that the cat had an inkling as to what he had done to its food. Taking charge, he stepped inside and closed the patio door. The cat could just stay outside.

Ivers walked into the front room where he deposited himself in his favorite reclining chair. He picked up his glasses and a book, kicked off his slippers and began to read. A few minutes later, his head dropped on his chest, and he fell asleep.

Sometime later, Ivers awoke with a start. It was dark outside, and he hadn't turned on any lights in the house. He stood and turned on the lamp next to his chair. He wandered down the hall, turning on lights as he went. He made a quick stop in the bathroom and then entered the kitchen.

He realized that he had stepped on something gooey and

moved his foot to see what it was. It was cat poop. Oh no! He had forgot to lock the cat doors into the garage and house. Snookums was on the loose in the house, leaving its feces wherever it wanted. What a catastrophe!

Grumbling, Ivers scooted carefully to the kitchen sink where he wet a paper towel and wiped the excrement off the bottom of his foot. He flicked on more lights, grabbed the pooper scooper and a handful of wet wipes. He then cleaned the mess on the kitchen floor.

"Snookums, where are you," he called softly as he tried to lure the cat to him. He waited, but the cat was too smart for him.

Shaking the container of cat treats, Ivers cooed, "I have treats for you."

Still, the cat did not respond.

With a heavy sigh, Ivers began his room-to-room search through the house for the cat and its droppings. He returned to the front room and was stunned to see that the cat had left a present for him on his favorite chair. Angrily, he walked over and picked up the dropping with the pooper scooper and wiped off the residue from his chair.

He found several more droppings in the hallway that he cleaned up. He went to the bedroom and threw on the light. Yep, there was another stool on the queen-sized bed. Of course, it was on his side. With a grim look on his face, he cleaned up the mess.

Afterward, he traversed the house looking for the cat, but Snookums was nowhere to be found. He went into the garage where he deposited his odorous findings into the trash can.

As he turned, he spotted a dust-covered Super Soaker Water Blaster. He walked to the shelf and picked it up. He took it inside the house and washed it at the kitchen sink before filling it with water and pumped the cylinder to build pressure in the gun.

Ivers turned on the outside patio light and slid open the patio door. Stepping outside, he tested the gun. It didn't disappoint him. It still had its firing power. Ivers was pleased as he started to go back inside the house. That's when he spotted Snookums. The cat had walked through the cat door from the garage and was sitting, with a pleased countenance, on the patio.

"Oh, baby Snookums. Come to Daddy. Daddy has a surprise for you," Ivers called softly as he tried to entice the cat to approach him. Instead, the cat remained immobile. It just stared at Ivers as it licked the side of its mouth.

Ivers slowly began to raise the Super Soaker Water Blaster. That's when the cat sensed danger and scampered across the yard. Ivers sent a couple of futile blasts of water at the fast-moving cat but missed. He saw the cat's rear end disappear under the fence. It knew what Ivers was going to do and hightailed it next door.

Ivers set the squirt gun on the patio table and reentered the house, closing the patio door behind him. He would have his revenge the next time he spotted Snookums. He locked the cat door from the garage to the house so that Snookums wouldn't be able to return inside and do more damage during the night.

He returned the wet wipes to the shelf and yawned. It had been a day filled with misadventures, the old man thought as he padded down the hallway to his bedroom. He was tired. Yawning, he unlocked the front window and opened it a few inches so that the fresh evening air could enter the room.

He shucked off his clothes and climbed into bed, wearing only his undershorts. Since his wife wasn't there, he didn't have her nagging him to change into pajamas, brush his teeth or use bacteria-fighting mouthwash.

He spread out on the bed since he had it all to himself. While he quickly fell asleep, he woke up in a cold sweat several times during the night due to a recurring, haunting dream. He couldn't get rid of the recurring nightmare that made him feel guilty and helpless. They had been a nightly occurrence for several years.

CHAPTER 3

Tuesday Morning

Kicking off his blankets, Ivers rolled out of bed and made a visit to the bathroom to shower. After he pulled on a green polo shirt and gray slacks, he went down the hall to the kitchen. As he walked past the patio door, he heard a noise on the screen. It was Snookums, who had climbed up on the screen patio door to get his attention.

Snickering as he remembered that the cat spent the night outside, Ivers slid open the glass part of the patio door.

"Were you outside all night?" he asked merrily.

Snookums gave him a death stare as if asking, "How could you?"

"Hang on a moment," Ivers said as he turned away while laughing at his pun. He looked around for the Super Soaker, then remembered it was outside on the patio table. He walked over to the kitchen sink and poured himself a small glass of water.

Sipping it, he returned to the cat hanging on the screen door. "I've told you I don't like you climbing on that screen. You're making holes in it," he said before suddenly emptying the remaining contents of his water glass on the cat.

With a screech, the cat released its grip and jumped to the patio where it disappeared around the corner. Ivers chuckled and was pleased with his action, something he wouldn't have dared to do when his wife was home. He made himself a couple of pieces of toast and a cup of coffee for breakfast.

Since it was another warm Southport day, he ambled onto the patio where he placed his breakfast on the metal table and sat on one of the firm patio chairs. Munching on his toast, he enjoyed the saltwater breeze from the nearby Atlantic. He scanned the yard for the cat and spotted it near the shed in the far corner of the fenced yard. It was glaring at Ivers.

After finishing breakfast, Ivers headed to his bedroom where he changed into a pair of brief, white workout shorts. He planned to work out and surprise his wife with a six-pack rather than the beer barrel he fronted currently. Before he could start lifting his ten-pound weight, the front doorbell rang.

Frowning at the interruption, Ivers went quickly to the front door where he peered through the peephole. He didn't see anyone and guessed that a package was delivered. He threw the door wide open where he was greeted by an unexpected visitor.

It was the five-year-old daughter of his across-the-street neighbor, Jill Tracy. Tracy, who was an assistant prosecutor for the city, was standing at the end of Ivers' driveway. Ivers always tried to be nice to her as he didn't want any trouble with the law.

"Hello, Thea," Ivers said as he bent down to talk to the child.

Thea's eyes bugged out as she stared at Ivers. She turned and called to her mother. "Mom, Mr. Ivers is naked!"

Panic filled Ivers as he quickly stepped onto the porch so that Tracy could see him. With one hand on the front door to keep it from shutting and locking him out, he shouted, "Jill, I'm not naked. I'm in my gym shorts to work out."

Tracy couldn't hide her amusement as she allowed a large smile to cross her face. "I can see that George," she shouted.

Ivers turned his attention back to Thea. "What can I do for you, honey?"

Thea was wary as she eyed Ivers' attire. Somewhat bashfully, she held up a partially empty box of candy bars. "I'm selling candy bars for my preschool. Would you want one?"

Ivers looked at the box and made a quick decision. "I'll take the remaining three. What do I owe you?"

"They're ten dollars each," Thea beamed, quite proud that she now had sold the entire box of candy bars.

Grimacing at the high price of the candy bars, the usually thrifty Ivers replied, "Let me get my wallet. I'll be right back."

He grumbled to himself to the bedroom and back. Pulling the thirty dollars out of his wallet, he handed them to Thea and took the three candy bars. He was even more upset to see that they were dark chocolate. He didn't like dark chocolate.

"Thank you, Mr. Ivers," a smiling Thea said as she bounded off the porch and returned to her mother's side.

"Thank you, George," Tracy called as the two turned to walk across the street.

Ivers closed the front door and leaned against it. He was overcome by mixed emotions of how he had narrowly avoided being an exhibitionist in front of the assistant city prosecutor and the amount of money he had just wasted on candy he didn't like.

Frustrated, Ivers returned to his bedroom and placed the candy bars on his wife's dresser to surprise her when she returned. Turning away from his original idea of working out, he changed back into his polo shirt and slacks. They were much safer attire he thought as he pulled his suspenders over his shoulder.

He walked down the hallway and out to his patio where he was greeted by the sound of someone pounding away on drums. The noise originated next door in the Bishops' backyard. Narrowing his eyebrows, Ivers wondered why he was being tormented by the noise. He then remembered Hudson telling him that he got a new drum set. He must be the one playing the drums, Ivers thought.

An evil smile crossed Ivers' face. He walked over to the spigot on the back of the house and turned on the water. Grabbing the hose, he unraveled it as he walked over to his side of the solid wood fence. He picked a spot that was on the other side of the beating drum. Turning on the spray pattern, he aimed the hose over the fence, snickering at the thought of drenching Hudson.

"Hey Mr. Ivers, your hose is pointed over the fence!" a voice called from the back corner of Ivers' garage.

Ivers turned to identify the source of the voice although he had an uneasy feeling that he knew who it was. At the same time, Phyllis shrieked next door.

"My hair! My hair. I'm drenched!" she cried as the drumbeats ceased abruptly. "Jack, tell George to turn off his sprinkler. It's coming right over our fence," she directed as she scurried inside her house to dry off.

A very uncomfortable look appeared on Ivers' face as he realized that he had doused her with the water. He felt a surge of panic and guilt, but also a hint of amusement. He wondered if he should apologize or pretend nothing happened.

As he shut off the nozzle, Hudson yelled, "Mr. Ivers, you got my grandma all wet." The youngster tried to hide his glee but wasn't successful.

At the same time, Ivers heard something striking the side of the fence. Jack had placed a ladder against the fence and climbed it to peer over at Ivers.

"George, did you know you just watered my wife?"

"It was an accident, Jack. The hose got away from me,"

Ivers explained quickly.

Jack had a skeptical look on his face. "Are you sure it didn't have anything to do with her playing Hudson's new drums?"

"Oh no. I was enjoying it," Ivers said as he tried to cover his true intentions. "As a matter of fact, I was hoping you'd play more," he said eagerly, trying to placate his neighbor.

"Why George, that's mighty nice of you. I'll get the drums dried off and Hudson can beat on it as much as he wants. I'll even get out my guitar and speakers. We'll turn it up real high so you can enjoy it. Got to go, buffalo." Jack's head disappeared as he climbed down the ladder.

Ivers grimaced. He turned around to talk to Hudson, but the boy had disappeared. Grabbing the hose, he began pulling it back to the house. Suddenly, a stream of cold water hit Ivers' back, soaking him amidst Hudson's giggles. Ivers turned and saw Hudson. He had climbed the ladder that Jack had left leaning against the fence and was holding a hose while directing its cold stream of water at Ivers.

"Got you back," Hudson giggled as Ivers scooted out of its range, returning to the patio.

"Hope you enjoyed the water," Jack called from the other side of the fence as he helped Hudson to the ground and turned off the nozzle.

Ten minutes later, Ivers had changed into dry clothes and returned to the patio. He sat in his chair to enjoy the second nice day in a row. Quickly, the air became filled with someone hammering on a drum set and someone else loudly playing a guitar. Ivers thought there was a violation of the noise code.

Jack's singing sounded like a cat being strangled by a rusty chain. He belted out tunes from the 80's and 90's with no regard for pitch, rhythm, or lyrics. He'd make up his own words when he didn't know the original ones, and they were usually worse than the original ones. When he began singing, "I'm a Barbie girl, in a Barbie world," Ivers walked inside the house.

After the terrible music finally ended, Ivers felt a surge of relief and joy. He had suffered through two hours of the most atrocious sounds ever produced by human beings and was ready to celebrate his survival. He shuddered at the thought of it resuming the next day. He decided to be on his best behavior so as not to incite them to repeat it.

Carefully sliding open the glass patio door, Ivers paused to listen. It was quiet. He smiled as he walked onto the patio and headed for the shed. He needed to start that riding mower so he could go to town for groceries. The mower had been idle since his wife contracted a lawn service to take care of their lawn.

The old white shed in the back of the yard needed some of the wood replaced and a new paint job. A few shingles were missing from the roof and there was green mold creeping up its north side.

Ivers swung open the two doors that squeaked at being moved. Looking inside, he saw his riding mower. It hadn't been started in a long time. Next to it was a cart that he pulled behind it. There was an empty space next to the cart.

That's where he parked his three-wheel bicycle. He no longer had it. A month ago, he had ridden it to the store a few blocks away and crashed into the side of a police car, damaging the car fender and destroying the bike. He had been cited and the bike was totaled. He was lucky in that he only suffered a few bruises.

Beyond that empty space was a pile of junk that no one ever bothered to sort through: old tools, broken furniture, rusty cans, and dusty books. The cobweb-infested shed was home to various critters such as mice, spiders, chipmunks and squirrels.

Ivers climbed onto the riding mower and saw the key was still in the ignition. He pushed the choke lever forward a couple of times and turned the key. The 18-horsepower engine roared as it started, and Ivers smiled. Maybe the day was taking a turn for the better.

Without hesitation, Ivers stepped on the accelerator, and the mower jumped backward, crashing into the cart parked behind it. A wide-eyed Ivers slammed on the brake, then looked down at the shifter.

He had forgot to check it. It was set in reverse. Ivers rolled his eyes at his mistake and put it in the forward position. He drove the mower out of the shed and turned it off while he pulled the cart out. Of course, the cart had a low tire.

Ivers returned to the shed, tripping his way around the tangle of tools on the floor to find a tire pump. Returning to the cart, he pumped up the tire then closed the shed. He hooked up the cart to the riding mower and drove to the house. He walked into the house to get a glass of sweet tea and his wallet in preparation for his afternoon trek to the convenience store several blocks away.

CHAPTER 4

Tuesday Afternoon

Grabbing his worn straw hat, Ivers was ready for his next adventure, a sunny afternoon ride to the convenience store. He left the house and opened the gate on the other side of the garage. He then mounted his riding mower and started it. He revved up the engine, which sounded like a dying cat, and headed around the garage down to the sidewalk with the cart in tow.

He turned onto the sidewalk and moved briskly toward the store as he enjoyed his freedom. He allowed himself to imagine that the mower was a Harley, and he was the leader of the pack. It was the most fun he enjoyed in the last 24 hours.

The ride along the live oak-lined street was like driving through a tunnel created by a canopy of green leaves and twisted branches that helped block out the sun. The air was filled with the sounds of rustling leaves and chirping birds. The serene neighborhood exemplified the charm of the South. Majestic.

Two blocks later, Ivers emerged from the tunnel-like drive as he entered the Southport business district with its stores for tourists. The sidewalk became crowded, and he drove onto the street, turning right on Davies Street, then left on East Nash Street. He had avoided the intersection of East Moore Street and Howe Street.

Ivers reached the store on Howe Street after ten minutes and parked his mower in front of the entrance next to a shiny sports car. He walked in with a swagger, feeling proud of himself as he grabbed a shopping cart. He was going to buy whatever he wanted to eat since he didn't have his wife to monitor him. This was going to be a real treat, Ivers thought as he headed to the aisle with candy and chips. First things first, he thought.

Ivers tossed a bunch of sugar-infused snacks in the cart before adding lunch meat, bread, hot dogs, chocolate milk, pastries, a chocolate cake, and two boxes of Twinkies and Hostess cupcakes. As he headed for checkout, he stopped suddenly. Quickly turning his back, he was able to dodge his neighbor Phyllis who walked by the end of the aisle. He didn't need her to be a tattletale informing on him to his wife.

He peeked around the end of the aisle and saw her going the other way. Moving fast, he went to the cashier.

"Hello George. We haven't seen you in a long time," the store owner Larry Sams greeted Ivers. "Usually, Charlotte does the shopping."

"She's out of town," Ivers responded.

As Sams rang up Ivers' items, he smiled, "I knew something was different. I don't see Charlotte buying items like these."

"And don't you tell her," Ivers glared.

Laughing, Sams winked, "That's okay George. We can keep it just between us boys."

"And don't tell Phyllis Bishop when she checks out. I saw her in one of the aisles," Ivers pleaded. "She'd call Charlotte right away and spill the beans."

"Got you covered."

"Larry, do you still have that soft serve ice cream?"

"We do. Would you like me to add a small cone to your bill?" Sams asked.

Ivers didn't respond right away. He was eyeing the sizes of the cones on display. "I'll take a large waffle cone with vanilla ice cream."

"Hi, Mr. Ivers," a voice piped up from next to Ivers.

Ivers looked down and frowned. It was Hudson.

"You sure are buying a lot of goodies, Mr. Ivers. Do you want to share? My grandmother says it's always nice to share." The words poured out of the youngster's mouth in a torrent.

"Listen Hudson," Ivers started as he bent down toward Hudson. "How about I buy you an ice cream cone and you keep this a secret between you and me?"

"Okay. Chocolate." The boy's eyes widened with glee as his head bobbed up and down.

"Larry, can you add a small chocolate cone to the bill?" Ivers asked.

"No. I want a big waffle cone like you, Mr. Ivers," Hudson countered.

Ivers grimaced at the extra cost. "Go ahead Larry. Make his a waffle cone, too."

Ivers paid his bill and had Hudson help him carry the bags of groceries outside to the cart. They returned inside to get their cones before going back outside and sitting on a bench in the building's shade.

"Good thing I saw you today, Mr. Ivers," Hudson said between licks of his tasty treat.

"Why is that, Hudson?"

"I got to have ice cream with you," he beamed at his newfound friend.

Wrinkling his nose at the thought of them being buddies, Ivers had a fiendish idea. He turned to the boy and suggested, "Hudson, let's have a race and see who can eat their ice cream the fastest."

"I can do that!" Hudson grinned at the challenge. He switched from licking to biting large chunks of ice cream.

"Oh no. It looks like you're going to beat me," Ivers commented in a semi-serious worried tone as he watched the boy gulping down his ice cream.

It quickly began to hit Hudson as he took big bites of the cold and creamy ice cream, ignoring the warning signs of his body. He felt a sharp pain in his forehead, like someone had stabbed him with a needle. He stopped eating and clutched his head, groaning. He had a brain freeze!

"Are you okay? You don't look so well," Ivers said with feigned concern.

"I've got brain freeze!" Hudson moaned as he rubbed his head.

"Press your tongue against the roof of your mouth. That should help," Phyllis instructed Hudson. The two had been so focused on eating their ice cream that they didn't notice she had walked out of the store with a bag of groceries.

"Thanks Grandma," Hudson grimaced in pain as he did as she suggested.

"And you George Ivers, did you instigate this?" she demanded.

"Oh no. We were just sitting here and eating ice cream," Ivers responded with downcast eyes.

"We were racing to see who could eat theirs the fastest," Hudson interjected.

"George, you know better," she commented in a serious tone.

"I think it was kind of an accident," Ivers replied weakly. "How about I give Hudson a ride home in the cart behind my riding mower to make up for it?"

"Can I, Grandma? I feel better now. It would be so much fun to ride in that cart with all of the goodies Mr. Ivers bought," Hudson gushed as he recovered from the brain freeze.

Ivers groaned softly at hearing the comment about goodies.

"Let me see if there's room," Phyllis said as she walked over to the cart. She was really interested in seeing what the goodies were so she could call Charlotte and let her know that George wasn't following a good diet.

Finished with her inspection, she answered Hudson, "Yes. You can ride the cart home." She focused her eyes on Ivers. "That's straight home, George. No detours."

Nodding his head, Ivers responded, "Straight home. No detours. I got it."

Phyllis walked to her car and drove home, leaving the man and her grandson to finish their ice cream.

Hudson was now eating more slowly, causing Ivers to comment, "Look how much more I have left to enjoy since you ate yours so fast." He couldn't resist teasing the boy.

"Excuse me. Would you mind watching my dog while I grab a couple of things from the store?" a warm, feminine voice asked.

Ivers looked up and saw a striking, thirty-year-old blonde with big blue eyes in jogging attire leaning toward him. She was going to be someone who would be difficult to refuse.

He looked past her and saw a big, fluffy, golden retriever with a red bandana around its neck. It looked very friendly and happy, wagging its tail and panting.

"Sure," Hudson responded quickly before Ivers could answer. He walked over and scratched its ears while it licked his face. It kept wagging its tail and looking at him with its big, brown eyes.

"Thank you. Her name is Joni," she said as she handed the end of the leash to Hudson. "I'll just be a few minutes."

Ivers felt a mix of relief and annoyance. He didn't like dogs and was glad that Hudson took the responsibility. He also didn't have to say no to the lady. He watched as Hudson fed the dog what was left of his waffle cone.

Ivers watched as Hudson played with the dog on the grass next to the store. Barking, it jumped on him, knocking him over and began licking his face again. The two wrestled playfully as Ivers thought about pulling a prank on the lady about her dog. Thinking more wisely, he dismissed it.

Ivers saw the woman return with a shopping bag in one hand. She called out, "I hope Joni didn't cause any trouble for you."

"No. We had fun," Hudson said joyously as he handed the leash to the woman. He bent down and gave Joni a big hug before the two walked away. Joni, with a sad expression, looked back at Hudson. She seemed to say goodbye with her eyes.

"Ready to head home?" Ivers asked as he stood. He was ready to go. He headed for the riding mower and climbed aboard. Starting the engine, he asked again, "Hudson, ready to go?"

"Yes. All aboard," Hudson replied with a burst of energy. He climbed into the cart, and they began the ride back to Ivers' house.

If Ivers hadn't been so focused on driving the riding mower, he would have noticed something amiss in the cart. Hudson had discovered the chocolate cupcakes and Twinkies. He was hungry and, with eyes gleaming, decided to open the box of Twinkies first. He didn't think that Ivers would mind him taking just one. After all, he wanted to do a quality check on them to make sure that Ivers didn't have stale Twinkies.

The problem was that after eating one, he decided he better check one more, then one more, and one more. When the Twinkies were gone, he decided to taste the chocolate cupcakes.

He munched and gobbled the entire ride home.

Ivers pulled the riding mower to a stop in front of the Bishops' house. "I'll drop you here at your grandparents' house," Ivers said as he wanted to make sure the boy wouldn't be hanging out with him that evening.

As he turned to the boy in the cart, a look of surprise crossed his face. Hudson had chocolate frosting from the cupcakes around his lips. His eyes were half-closed, and his little cheeks were swollen like a chipmunk's.

"I don't feel so good, Mr. Ivers," he moaned.

Ivers' eyes went from the boy to the empty Twinkie and cupcake boxes before returning to glare at the boy. "You don't look so good either. I bet you're going to throw up," he grumbled angrily at the boy.

"Oh George, I see you brought Hudson home," Phyllis called as she stepped off the porch and approached them with her husband Jack following her. "How sweet of...," she began.

She stopped dead in her tracks as she saw the sickened look on Hudson's face and the ring of chocolate around his mouth. "Oh no, Sweetie. What happened to you?" she asked quickly as she raced to her grandson's side.

"I don't know. I think I ate something that doesn't agree with me," he groaned as he clutched his stomach where a storm was beginning to brew. It started with a rumble, then a grumble, followed by a tumble of regret. His belly, now a mixing bowl of sugary delights, was churning out complaints louder than a freight train. Hudson's face turned green as his stomach became queasier.

Reaching her hand to help him out of the cart, Phyllis spoke in a concerned tone, "We better get you inside before you start throwing up out here."

Stepping out of the cart, Hudson nodded his head in agreement. He knew what was coming next as they hustled toward the house.

"I'm sorry George. I'll replace the food he ate," Phyllis called over her shoulder as she ushered the young boy into the house, and the screen door shut behind her.

"Poor boy," Jack muttered as he turned from watching the door close to look at Ivers. "George, I heard you got pulled over for DWI," Jack said with a serious look on his face.

"What? I haven't had a drop all day, but that just might change when I walk into my home," Ivers grumbled.

Ignoring Ivers' response, Jack continued, "You know I was a bit concerned when I heard that Hudson got in that cart."

"You need to get your facts straight, Jack. I didn't get pulled over for any DWI!" Ivers snapped.

"Oh yes you did! DWI! That's driving while incontinent," Jack laughed as he walked away. "Can't stay, blue jay," Jack called over his shoulder. It was a good thing that Jack didn't turn around. He would have seen the death stare that Ivers threw at him.

Ivers was perturbed at Jack's crack. He was also disturbed that the boy had eaten his sweet treats. As he drove the riding mower next door to his home, he allowed an evil smile to cross his lips at the thought of the boy vomiting. He hoped he didn't make it to the bathroom. That would be payback for what the boy had done.

Ivers parked the riding mower behind the patio and closed the gate. He carried the remaining grocery bags into the house and set them on the counter.

After putting the groceries away and tossing the empty Twinkies and Hostess cupcake packages in the trash, Ivers proceeded to make himself a sandwich out of the lunch meat he bought. It was going to be turkey on rye with a big piece of chocolate cake for dessert and sweet tea.

Carrying the dinner to the table on the patio, he set it down and plopped into one of the sturdy metal chairs. While he relaxed and ate, he gazed at his tranquil back yard. It seemed so peaceful - almost. He saw Snookums prance into view. The mischievous feline sat 20 feet away from him and began to give itself a bath.

Ivers noticed the meticulous way it licked every inch of its fur, the contortions it made to reach the hard-to-get spots, and the occasional pause to nibble on a stubborn speck of dirt. It paused several times to stare at Ivers as if to say that you can never outsmart me.

Ivers was up to the challenge as his mind began to conjure up ways to get even with the cat for pooping throughout the house. He decided to outsmart the cat by setting up the lawn sprinkler.

After he finished eating, Ivers walked into the garage and found the worn sprinkler. It reminded him of himself - worn but still useful. He opened a cabinet near his workbench and found a motion detector.

Walking back to the patio, he unscrewed the nozzle from the hose and installed the motion detector, then screwed on the sprinkler. When he looked for the cat, it had disappeared.

Ivers grinned as he realized that the cat wouldn't see him set his trap. He placed the sprinkler where Snookums had been bathing itself. He then returned to the patio and turned on the water. Walking back toward the sprinkler, he tested the motion detector, and it immediately activated the sprinkler, sending water twirling through the air.

Pleased with his trap, Ivers walked into the house and retrieved the box of kitty treats. When he returned to the patio, he called out, "Snookums. I have a treat for you!" He shook the box several times to entice the cat to appear. He repeated the calls several times with no results. He sat down in his chair and waited, but the cat did not appear.

Frustrated with his lack of success and the growing darkness of an early evening, Ivers reentered the house and headed for his bedroom. After opening the bedroom window, he stripped to his undershorts and climbed into bed. It had been a long day, and it would be nice to have the bed all to himself.

Well, almost all to himself as the cat jumped up on the bed before Ivers shut off the lamp on the nightstand. It must have come inside through the cat doors that he had unlocked earlier.

Snookums was accustomed to sleeping under the blanket in the secure arms of Charlotte. The cat looked for Charlotte but found itself staring into the unwelcome glare from Ivers' narrowed eyes.

"Not tonight, Snookums," Ivers grumbled as he swatted at the cat who jumped off the bed. He could see that the cat's fur was dry, meaning it hadn't triggered the sprinkler. "Maybe Friday night after Charlotte returns," Ivers stated firmly as he turned off the lamp and settled on his side. Within minutes, he fell into a deep sleep. Meanwhile, Snookums curled into a ball on the floor and drifted off.

CHAPTER 5

Wednesday Morning

Opening his eyes, Ivers sat up in the bed and stretched his arms toward the ceiling as he yawned. His sleep had been interrupted as usual by the recurring nightmares. They were so frustrating for Ivers, who wished he could shake them off.

Ivers slowly swung his legs over the side of the bed and stood. He was unaware that Snookums was sleeping next to his side of the bed. He next heard a high-pitched "MEOOOW!" shatter the silence of the dawn as he unintentionally had stepped on the cat's tail. Startled, Ivers hopped on one foot, then the other, in a comical dance that would have made a ballerina envious.

Snookums, with its tail fluffed up like a bottlebrush, darted out of the room with the speed of a rocket. Ivers, now fully awake and more agile than he'd felt in years, couldn't help but chuckle with glee at the thought of interrupting the snoozing cat's sleep. He just didn't like that cat.

He ambled into the bathroom to complete his usual morning routine before dressing for the day. He then went to the kitchen where he made coffee and toast covered with a thick layer of strawberry jam.

As he ate on the patio, Ivers allowed his eyes to run along the fence line between his house and the Bishops' house. He spotted a hornet nest hanging from one of the lower branches of the live oak next to the shed at the rear of the property. It was a breeding ground for trouble as Ivers was soon to learn first-hand.

He decided to walk back to the hornet nest and inspect it.

As he walked, he heard the sprinkler kick on a second before it sprayed him with water. He was so absent-minded that he forgot that he had set it on a motion detector the previous day. Jumping back before he became drenched, Ivers returned to the house and shut off the faucet. He then resumed his trek to the hornet nest.

He closely examined it as the hornets flew in and out. They remained active since Southport hadn't incurred a hard freeze yet. They were so busy that they made ants look lazy, Ivers cracked quietly to himself. He decided it would be a good idea to get rid of the hornets, especially since his wife had asked him several weeks ago.

Ivers walked over to the shed and opened the door. He entered the dingy, cluttered shed to locate the extra length of hose that was stored there. Grabbing it, he walked back to the house where he disconnected the sprinkler and connected the extra hose on the patio. He stretched it out and was pleased to see that it easily reached the area beneath the hornet nest so that he could drown them by spraying it.

He returned to the house and turned on the spigot. When he started to walk back to the other end of the hose, a look of dismay crossed his face as he beheld a sad sight. The old leaky hose lay on the grass, limp and lifeless. Water dripped from its many holes, forming puddles on the ground. Ivers shook his head sadly from side to side as he remembered using the weed eater too close to the hose several months earlier.

He walked back to the spigot and turned off the water, then pulled the two hoses to the patio where he disconnected the bad hose. He carried it around the corner of the garage and put it in the trash container.

Ivers next returned to the shed where he looked around for

something to use to get rid of the hornets. He saw a baseball bat in the corner but quickly dismissed the idea of swinging at the nest as if it was a piñata.

He spotted his old Bernzomatic soldering torch kit on the small workbench. It had a trigger-start torch head attached to a 14-ounce propane cylinder. Smiling at the thought of burning out the pesky intruders with his miniature flamethrower, he picked it up and pulled the trigger. Nothing. He pulled the trigger several more times with no results. He threw the torch on the workbench in frustration and began to scan the shed for something else to use.

His eyes rested on his old five-gallon wet/dry shop vacuum. It had been replaced a year earlier with a new one that his wife gifted him for Christmas. With a renewed sense of purpose, he dug it out of the far corner and rolled it outside. He returned to the garage where he located his reel with the extra-long extension cord. Plugging one end into the patio outlet, he walked back to the vacuum where he connected it to the cord.

Flicking the switch, he was quite pleased that the vacuum still worked. He switched it back off, then attached the two plastic extension wands to the seven-foot hose.

"What are you doing Mr. Ivers? You going to vacuum the yard?" Hudson's voice called from the fence.

Ivers turned and saw that the young boy's head was peering over the fence top at him. He had apparently placed a ladder against the fence so that he could see what was happening in Ivers' yard.

Ivers didn't want to talk, nor did he want anyone watching him work. "I was just testing it to make sure it works," he called. "Why don't you go practice your drums?"

Hudson's face beamed. "You like my drum playing? I don't

know what I'm doing yet."

I can tell, Ivers muttered under his breath before commenting, "Oh no. I think you have it down. Go ahead and play them for me."

"Okay." Hudson's head disappeared and moments later, the sound of him pounding on the drums filled the air.

Ivers reentered the shed and picked up some old newspapers and a pack of matches. He carried them outside and placed them on the ground below the hornet nest. He started a fire and placed some recent grass clippings on top of them. Smoke soon waffled upwards toward the hornet nest.

Ivers ran over to the vacuum and switched it on, then returned to the hornet nest with the vacuum in tow. He stuck the end of the wand into the nest and grinned as he heard the hornets being sucked inside the canister.

Suddenly a streak of water struck Ivers' pant leg and the fire. With a look of consternation, he followed the stream to its source. Hudson, who had climbed the ladder again, was holding a hose directed at the fire.

"Mr. Ivers, you almost caught yourself on fire. Did you know that you had a fire next to you?"

Ivers felt like steam was emitting from his ears as he fought to control his anger.

When Hudson loosened his grip on the hose, it began to writhe and twist like a serpent awakened from its slumber. The hose drenched Ivers who, in turn, appeared to be dancing a clumsy jig as he tried to dance out of its range.

From the safety of the dry patio, Snookums watched with wide-eyed amusement. It had the best seat in the house as its tail twitched with delight at Ivers' wet predicament. This was better than a catnip-induced high.

When the water-soaked and almost breathless Ivers turned and took two steps toward the fence, he stumbled over the vacuum power cord, disconnecting the vacuum from its power source.

Quickly turning around, he saw the end of the vacuum shoved up the hornet nest, but it no longer was sucking hornets into the vacuum. Instead, angry hornets were emerging from the bottom of the nest. Several headed toward Ivers, who dropped the vacuum wand and scooted as fast as he could toward the safety of the house, swatting hornets on the way. His unique movements as he ran looked as if he was trying out as a performer for Riverdance.

Slamming the screen sliding door behind him, he rubbed a couple of the hornet stings on his arm while he surveyed the backyard. Laughter was coming from the fence where Hudson and Jack, who had joined him after shutting off the water, were enjoying Ivers' antics.

"I bet you got a good buzz out of that adventure," Jack giggled. "George, water doesn't kill hornets. Their wings dry off fast, then they attack you."

Ivers responded with a grimace.

"What are you going to do with that canister full of angry hornets? You probably voided your warranty," Jack called. "Hey George, do you know what sound a hornet makes when it goes splat on your windshield? A bee-flat! Bye-bye, butterfly," Jack added as he disappeared down the ladder.

Of course, Hudson had to jump in on the exchange. "Mr. Ivers. Knock, knock."

"Who's there?"

"Bee."

"Bee who?"

"Beware of the hornets," Hudson roared with glee as he also climbed down the ladder.

In response, a sullen-faced Ivers shut the glass patio door and pulled the curtain across. He was finished listening for advice from his neighbor.

A loud "meow" that suspiciously sounded like a chuckle to Ivers' ears emitted from Snookums who had darted inside with the sputtering and gasping man.

"You thought that was funny, huh?" Ivers barked as he glared at the cat.

Snookums reacted by purring with satisfaction.

CHAPTER 6

Wednesday Afternoon

After lunch, Ivers decided to relax. Carrying a book and a glass of sweet tea, he walked onto the patio and plopped into one of the chairs. He planned on enjoying a quiet afternoon after such a disruptive morning.

He allowed his eyes to gaze at the hornet nest, still hanging from the live oak branch. Maybe, he'd try to cut it loose that night and toss it into the Bishops' yard, he thought with a wicked grin. The weather report indicated the temperature would be dropping and that meant the hornets wouldn't be as active.

Buttoning his sweater as the air chilled, he slipped on his eyeglasses and picked up his book. A smile crossed his face at the thought of no distractions, although he did cock his head to the side to be sure he didn't hear Jack on his guitar or Hudson on the drums. Satisfied that nothing was amiss, he focused on his book. The quiet would soon end.

No more than five minutes later, Ivers heard someone pounding on something, the noise shattering what had been a peaceful afternoon. He looked toward the Bishops' yard, but it didn't seem to be coming from there. Wrinkling his brow in wonderment, he resumed reading.

The pounding persisted. Ivers stood and listened. It seemed like it was originating from the front of his house. Must be the town street crew at work, Ivers thought as he stood from his chair. A brisk breeze was picking up as he moved inside the house.

Setting the book and sweet tea on the counter, he walked over to the thermostat and turned up the heat, then entered the bathroom. When he finished, he flushed the toilet and watched the water as it swirled down the toilet bowl. It reminded him of his life - going down the toilet.

While he was washing his hands, the front doorbell rang. He ambled to the door and opened it. Standing in front of him was Hudson, who was holding a hammer and chisel.

"Hi Mr. Ivers, I've got a surprise for you."

With a theatrical roll of his eyes, Ivers inquired, "What's that, Hudson?"

"Remember the spots of paint that were on your front porch? I got rid of them for you."

Ivers' expression morphed into one of concern as his gaze darted to the porch. The once smooth concrete now resembled the surface of the moon. His eyes bulged, and his mouth hung agape as he uttered in disbelief, "What have you done?"

"I chipped them out for you," the well-intentioned boy said proudly as he showed off his handiwork.

The muscles in Ivers' face twitched as he fought to control his temper. He couldn't wait for the kid's visit with his grandparents to end. Frowning, Ivers spoke in a serious tone, "Hudson, I don't want you to do anything to my property without checking with me first. In fact, I don't want you to do anything, period!"

"Oh," Hudson acknowledged sadly.

"You understand?"

"Yes, but I did one more thing," Hudson spoke slowly, not wanting to reveal what else he had done.

Ivers' head snapped around as he surveyed the front of the house and the front yard. Not seeing anything, he asked reluctantly, "What else did you do?"

"Come on out front," the boy said warily.

Ivers placed the small wood block between the front door and door frame, then followed Hudson to the front yard.

"Do you like my sign? I thought you'd be glad that I made it for you." The boy pointed toward the porch railing.

Hesitantly, Ivers began to turn around. His eyes widened once again as he saw a black ink-scrawled, cardboard sign nailed to the white railing. It read "Do Not Disturd." Ivers began to chuckle despite himself.

Hearing Ivers, Hudson beamed, "You like it?"

"It is very appropriate," Ivers snickered.

"I knew you'd like it," a relieved Hudson remarked with a newfound sense of confidence. "I made it myself. I bet you didn't know I won my class spelling bee contest," he gleamed.

A shiver ran up Ivers' back as the sky clouded and the temperature continued to drop. "Let's go inside."

Hudson entered first as Ivers moved the wood block away from the door and closed it after him. Ivers walked into the kitchen where he spotted Hudson on the floor next to Snookums. He was petting the purring cat.

Seeing Ivers, Hudson reached inside his pants pocket and pulled out a can of Play-Doh. "Mr. Ivers, have you ever played with Play-Doh?" he asked as he held up the can.

"A long time ago, I did," Ivers said as he watched the boy pull out a couple of Play-Doh stencils.

A symphony of clanks and hisses, followed by a growling noise, suddenly emitted through the basement door. The din came from the shadowy depths of the basement. Hudson's eyes bulged with fear, mirroring his ballooning terror. "What was that?" he asked, his voice trembling like a leaf in the wind.

Ivers knew immediately but decided to explain the noise in his own way. "That's the monster in my basement."

"Really? You really have a monster down there?" the boy asked as his voice quivered with trepidation.

A high-pitched shriek echoed off the basement concrete walls before Ivers answered. "Yes, and that's the sound it makes when it's hungry. Do you want to go downstairs with me to check? Are you brave enough?" Ivers asked as he feigned a serious look on his face.

Hudson looked down at his can of Play-Doh. "No. You can go ahead. I was just getting ready to play with this Play-Doh," Hudson explained quickly as the aluminum pipes creaked from the heat passing through them.

"Are you sure? I can give you a baseball bat to carry if you like," Ivers added.

Wrinkling his brow as he felt the room warming up, Hudson asked, "Were you teasing me, Mr. Ivers? Is that just your furnace?"

Frowning at the notion that his prank had failed, Ivers commented reluctantly, "Yes. It is. I had you fooled for a second, didn't I?"

"Maybe for just a second," Hudson agreed with relief.

"How would you like to go sledding?" Ivers asked as another idea popped into his head.

"Sledding? There's no snow. We can't go sledding," Hudson countered.

"Oh yes, we can. You sit right there, and I'll get you a sled." Ivers disappeared into the garage. When he returned several minutes later, he had a sheet of cardboard in his hands.

"That's not a sled," Hudson stated as he saw the cardboard.

"It will do. Come over here," Ivers said as he led the boy to the basement door and opened it. He switched on the light for the stairs and set the sheet of cardboard on the floor.

"All you have to do is sit on this cardboard and ride it down the steps," Ivers explained.

Hudson's face filled with skepticism as he looked at the cardboard and down the stairs. "Have you done this before?"

"Oh yeah. We did it all of the time when I was a kid."

Just then the basement behemoth roared, causing Hudson to take a step back. "That is the furnace, right?" he asked with trepidation.

"Of course," Ivers assured him. "Get on. It will be fun."

"I'm not going to get hurt, am I? My grandmother wouldn't like that," Hudson asked in a cautionary tone.

"No. It will be fine."

"Okay then," Hudson said as he sat down on the cardboard which Ivers had placed near the edge of the top step.

"Pull the front of the cardboard back like a toboggan," Ivers urged.

"A what?" Hudson questioned as he took a deep breath of courage.

Ivers didn't respond. He just pushed the boy over the edge, and he flew down the steps on his homemade sled.

When Hudson crashed at the bottom of the steps, he rolled off the cardboard onto the concrete floor. Casting a quick glance around the spooky basement, he jumped to his feet.

"That was fun," he giggled as he picked up the cardboard and looked up at Ivers. "Can I do it again?"

"Sure. Come back up here." Ivers offered.

The boy didn't need any urging as the beastly furnace roared, sending him flying up the steps. He set the cardboard down but held off taking another ride down as he listened for the creature below to quiet. He then pushed off, again going down the stairs quickly.

This went on for about five rides before the boy tired of it. He set the cardboard down and asked, "What do we do now, Mr. Ivers?"

Ivers stuck out his index finger. "Pull my finger," Ivers instructed Hudson quietly.

"Oh no. I know that one, Mr. Ivers. We do that at school a lot," the boy smirked at not falling for the prank.

Ivers looked out the glass patio door and saw the darkening clouds overhead. "Looks like it's going to pour. You better run along to your grandparents' house before it starts."

"That's a good idea, Mr. Ivers. I don't want to get wet like you did earlier," Hudson grinned.

Ivers remembered seeing a gift from Snookums on the patio floor. "Hang on a second. I have something for you to take home."

"Really. What is it? Will I like it?" Hudson peppered Ivers with questions.

"I'm sure you will, but your grandmother will like it more," Ivers replied with a small chuckle. He stepped outside and returned within thirty seconds. In his hand, he held a paper plate. On the plate was a dead mouse.

"I know what that is; it's a dead mouse. You want me to take that home?" Hudson asked perplexed.

"It's really for your grandmother," Ivers said with a caring look on his face. Not really. He was faking it.

"I don't think that my grandmother is going to like that, Mr. Ivers," Hudson countered firmly.

"You don't understand. It's where you put it that makes a difference," he explained.

"Like to scare her? I'm not going to do that. She'll put me in time out," Hudson replied all-knowingly.

"Oh no. We don't want to scare her. We are going to surprise her with the sweet-smelling scent that a dead mouse can emit," Ivers suggested. "It will just fill the house."

Hudson sniffed at the mouse and wrinkled his nose. "That stinks."

"Of course it does right now. But you just put it in the microwave for five minutes and it will smell so good," Ivers said in a convincing tone. "Your grandmother will love you for doing that."

"Really?"

"Cross my heart. Don't let her see you carry it in the house or put it in the microwave. You don't want to ruin her surprise," Ivers said in a conspiratorial tone as he handed the plate with the mouse to the youngster.

"Okay," Hudson said as he took the plate, and Ivers escorted him to the front door.

"Be sure she doesn't see you carry it inside," Ivers cautioned Hudson again as the boy left with an eager look on his face. Ivers closed the front door and stood with his back to it as he guffawed at what was about to happen next door.

CHAPTER 7

Wednesday Evening

Under ominously darkening skies, the wind began picking up offshore as a tempest brewed over the ocean. It moved from a whisper to a ferocious howl, announcing its arrival as it moved onshore and up the Cape Fear River. The leaves of Southport's live oak trees rustled while the branches swayed in a turbulent dance choreographed by the gusts.

The scent of rain and brine filled the air, signaling the approaching storm. The tree limbs creaked and groaned as the gale intensified.

The clouds grumbled with thunder while bright flashes of lightning filled the sky as the storm unleashed its fury. The downpour was sudden and fierce with its plump and plentiful raindrops turning driveways into rivers and gardens into swamps. Tree limbs and debris fell into the yards and streets.

Inside his home, Ivers felt quite comfortable. He had made his supper, read a few chapters from a book and was now settled into his bed. It had been a relatively quiet evening for him in contrast to the disturbing events of the day.

He enjoyed listening to the storm outside even though its driving rain had made him lower his bedroom window to about an inch above the sill. He breathed in the fresh rain-filled air and pulled his blanket up to his chin as he rolled onto his side.

It was around midnight that Ivers' slumber was interrupted. He was nestled snugly in his bed, snoring loudly like the hum of a sawmill until a loud noise awoke him. His eyes popped open, as wide as saucers, and he lay there motionless as he tried to determine the source of the noise.

Now fully awake, Ivers considered the possibilities. Right away he dismissed the creaking from the furnace ductwork. No, the noise was much louder. Maybe the cat knocked over something in the house. Frowning at the disruption, he decided to investigate.

When Ivers swung his legs over the side of the bed, he noticed that the storm had abated and was now a gentle rainfall. He reached for his glasses which were perched precariously on the nightstand, then padded silently out of his bedroom.

He spotted his cane in the front room and grabbed it. In his mind, it transformed into a mighty sword as he brandished it through the air. Creeping down the corridor with the stealth of a cat, he pondered the possibility of a nocturnal intruder. This could be his moment, his debut as a superhero!

Deciding not to turn on any lights to alert any potential burglar that he was coming, he made his way through the familiar maze of furniture in each room as he searched for the source of the noise. He checked each window and every door to make sure that they were locked as he went room-by-room.

Perplexed by not identifying the source of the noise, he walked back to the front of the house. A fleeting shadow caught his peripheral vision. Spinning to face the potential threat, Ivers adopted a stance reminiscent of a martial arts master, hands poised and ready, as he unleashed a battle cry, "Kiai!" The cane was held high, ready to strike.

"Meow," was the response.

Frowning, Ivers switched on the hall light to find Snookums staring up at him. It was seated in front of the door and appeared to want to go outside. So much for being a hero that night, he thought as he set the cane against the sofa. Next, he opened the front door.

As the cat ran out, Ivers spotted a large tree limb that had fallen in his front yard. He decided to walk onto the porch for a better view. He flicked on the porch light but then he remembered he was dressed in only his undershorts. He flicked off the light so that he wouldn't be highlighted by it.

Bending down as he stepped out, he placed the small wood block so that the door wouldn't lock behind him. He then stepped onto the porch and walked over to the railing where the cat was looking toward the fallen branch. Yes, that was probably the source of the noise that had awakened him, Ivers concluded.

Suddenly a bright flash of lightning cracked like a thunderbolt nearby. The cat raced past Ivers and through the front door, accidentally knocking the wood block inside. Ivers began to laugh at the cat's reaction when he realized that the front door had swung shut with a resounding click that echoed in Ivers' sinking heart. He walked quickly to the door and jiggled the handle, but it was locked.

To make matters worse, Ivers saw a movement behind the front window in the living room. He moved toward it and saw that the cat had climbed up on the top of the sofa and was staring at him through the safety of the glass. From its perch, Snookums watched the ensuing comedy unfold. Its eyes glinted with mischief, and its whiskers twitched with barely contained glee.

Ivers had a look of bewilderment painted across his face as he patted down his pockets only to find them as empty as a politician's promises. No keys. He also noted he didn't have pants on, only his undershorts – and they didn't have pockets.

As Ivers' symphony of mutterings followed, the cat couldn't help but let out a soft, purring laugh as it swished its tail. The soft glow of the streetlamps provided enough light for Ivers to see through the window the cat's reactions to his plight.

With a grimace, he walked off the porch into the soft rain and began checking all of the windows and doors. They, of course, were locked which was no surprise since he had already checked every window for an intruder's access. With a look of disbelief plastered across his face, Ivers somberly retreated to the back covered patio.

The motion detector light on the patio wall provided light for him when he arrived under the patio. He grabbed a dry towel and wiped off his glasses, then toweled himself dry. He wondered if God was testing him for all those times he had given way to his angry nature. As he sat there, the rain subsided. It now was a softer pitter patter on the metal roof overhead.

Ivers then realized he hadn't checked his master bedroom window. He had left it cracked open if he remembered correctly. Maybe he could remove the screen, raise the window and climb inside. With a triumphant look on his face, he jumped up and walked to the door to the garage and grabbed the handle. It was still locked. Hearing a noise at the kitchen window, Ivers turned and saw Snookums staring at him. Or was it smirking at him?

"Get down from there!" he shouted. "You know you're not allowed on the sink or the kitchen counters," he bellowed.

The cat didn't move. It just began licking its paws.

Ivers, however, wasn't one to be easily defeated. He turned and shuffled through the back yard to the shed, hoping to find some tool, any tool, that could aid in his reentry. Alas, the shed was locked too, guarding its contents like a dragon hoarding its gold. With a sigh that could deflate a hot air balloon, Ivers returned to the patio and sat on the patio chair to contemplate his next move.

Time ticked by, and Ivers formed another idea. What was he thinking? He could use the patio chair as a step up to the bedroom window.

As a shiver ran down his back from the chilling temperature, he wrapped the towel around his shoulders. He needed more protection from the cold rain. He recounted the recently disposed inflatable pool. After retrieving it from the trash can, he then rummaged around in his wife's flowering kit.

He beamed when he discovered an old pair of flower trimming shears which he used to cut up the pool material. He simply made himself a cape-like covering to protect himself from the rain which again intensified.

With a bit of ingenuity and a flair for the dramatic, he transformed the handmade cape by punching a pair of holes in it, then threaded a found scrap of rope through them to secure his new accessory superhero-style around his neck.

He needed something to protect his bald head and soon discovered an old football helmet under the outdoor grill. Slipping it on, he felt a sense of power and achievement flow quickly through his veins. I shall overcome, he thought proudly.

Carrying the chair and the trimming shears and wearing his outrageous outfit, Ivers carefully made his underwear-clad way to the front of the house. It was a bit difficult to see with his glasses fogged as if he were in a steam room. That was resolved when he triggered the motion-detector light at the front corner of the house. He forgot that he also was basically unclothed, save for his white boxers.

He instantly was spotlighted in his underwear, cape and helmet. He snapped his head around to see if anyone was watching him. Who would be outside in weather like this, he thought thankfully.

With a determination that would rival a cat burglar, he approached the master bedroom window. It was slightly ajar as he earlier had left it. With a large grin, he placed the chair below the window. He next hoisted himself up with a grunt as he held onto the back of the chair.

He used his wife's shears to pry at the edge of the window screen. When he couldn't budge the screen, he snipped away at it to make an opening.

Grinning victoriously, Ivers pulled away the screen far enough to make a huge opening for himself. He reached through and slid the storm window open. As he began to enter, Ivers was surprised by an unexpected command on a loudspeaker and the strong beam of a spotlight being directed at him from the street.

"Put your hands in the air and get down from that chair!"

Ivers turned his head toward the street where he saw two policemen in rain gear standing next to their vehicle. Their guns were drawn.

"It's not what you think," Ivers protested as he eased himself to the ground and turned around. When he did, he saw porchlights in neighboring homes flick on. Oh boy, he thought. He didn't want to have the neighbors see him like this.

"You look like a cross between a football player and a superhero with that cape," one officer cracked as he looked at the geriatric burglar.

"I live here," Ivers yelled, defensively.

With a mix of professionalism and barely contained amusement, the officers holstered their weapons and approached Ivers.

"You always pull off home burglaries dressed in your undershorts?" one officer asked as he struggled to maintain his composure.

"I can explain," Ivers replied with a sheepish look.

"This, I can tell, is going to be good," the other officer commented as he waited expectantly and laughed softly at the absurdity of the alleged thief's outfit.

"This is my house and I locked myself out. I was just trying to get back inside," Ivers explained quickly as he saw several of the neighbors now gathering under their open umbrellas on the sidewalk in front of his house.

The first officer turned to the onlookers. "Can anyone vouch for this gentleman? Is this his house?"

"Yes. That's George's house," a woman's voice called from the porch next door.

Ivers recognized the voice right away. It was Phyllis Bishop. He frowned at her coming to his rescue. Now, his wife would know all about it.

"George, you should have told me that it was you trying to climb in the house. I didn't recognize you and called the police," she shouted from the porch.

"What made you come out of your house and see him?" the first officer asked.

"I heard a noise and decided to get up to see what it was. It was that tree branch in George's yard that I heard," Phyllis explained.

"Can I go inside now?" Ivers asked, anxious to put the evening's events behind him.

"Sure. I'll climb through the window for you and unlock the front door," the first officer said as he stepped on the chair and entered the open window.

Turning to the onlookers, Ivers yelled angrily, "Show's over! I hope you enjoyed it!" As the neighbors returned to their homes, Ivers and the second officer walked onto the dry porch.

The front door opened, and the first officer stepped out.

"Don't let the door close. It will lock me out again," Ivers stated quickly as he bent down and grabbed the small wood block, placing it between the door and the door frame.

"If that's the problem, you need to get that fixed," the first officer suggested as he looked at the wood block that kept the door open.

"Right," Ivers answered in a gruff manner.

"You could have avoided all of this ruckus by asking a neighbor for help. They could have called us, and we could have assisted you in getting back inside your home," the first officer commented.

"I don't like to trouble people. Besides, it's none of their business," Ivers grumbled as he stepped inside the doorway. Facing them while doffing the football helmet and cape, he mumbled, "Thank you."

As the two officers walked away, the second turned and grinned, "Next time, be sure that you don't get locked out in just your undershorts."

The two chuckled as they returned to their vehicle, not seeing Ivers glaring at them before slamming the door. He stormed into the kitchen to take out his ire on the cat.

Snookums seemed to instinctively know what was coming and couldn't be found. Ivers returned to his bedroom where he shucked his wet shorts and took a hot shower before settling in bed for the night.

CHAPTER 8

Thursday Morning

Yawning, Ivers rolled onto his left side. What a night, he thought as he reached for his spectacles. Putting them on, he stared in surprise at the time on his alarm clock - 10:00 a.m. That was so out of character for him to sleep that late. With a groan, he sat up and swung his legs over the side of the bed. He headed for the bathroom and completed his usual morning routine.

As he finished, he heard the doorbell ring. In case it was Thea from across the street, he quickly slipped on his trousers and a T-shirt before adjusting his suspenders. He wasn't taking any chances on repeating the incident from a couple of days ago. Expecting perhaps the mailman or another of those pesky door-to-door salespeople, he certainly did not anticipate who was on the other side of the door.

When he opened the creaky front door, his face filled with a blank stare as he looked at the two people standing in front of him. Ivers pinched himself to see if he was dreaming as he stared at the duo. Standing in front of him were two twenty-some-year-olds. Gen Z for sure. One had spiked green hair and the other had purple hair that was cut Mohawk-style.

"Wrong house. You want the Bishops next door. I think she's changing her hair color to bright blue today," Ivers groused before slamming shut the door.

Before he could walk away, the doorbell began to ring incessantly. Now fully awake and realizing this was no dream, he reopened the door. Ivers really didn't want to talk to two fruit loops. He shouted at the colorful intruders, "I don't know what you're selling, but go away! I'm not buying anything!"

"Oh no," the green-haired one protested. "We're not from around here."

Looking each one of them up and down, Ivers spoke firmly to the two out-of-this-world creatures, "Apparently. This is planet Earth. I am an earthling!"

Surmising that they were dealing with a senior citizen who was very set in his intolerant ways and living in a past culture, they ignored his outbursts.

"We're the Raymonds; I'm Ody," green-hair explained.

"And I'm Dodie," Mohawk added.

"And you two clowns just escaped from the circus, didn't you?" Ivers growled.

"That's funny," Dodie observed.

"No. We just moved in two doors down," Ody stated with a smile.

"Why didn't you move two states down instead? You would be a perfect fit for Georgia," Ivers groused, trying to figure out where this conversation was headed. He really didn't want an exchange with these two characters.

They smiled.

"We brought freshly-baked cookies to greet our new neighbors," Ody said as she held out a paper plate with six cookies.

Ivers eyed the cookies suspiciously. "You put some of that illegal marijuana in those, didn't you?"

"No," Ody laughed. "Just mushrooms."

"They're magical," Dodie added.

Ivers looked down the street, then back at the couple in front of him. "You baked these?"

"Yes. Well, Dodie did," the shy Ody replied.

Ivers looked down the street again. "I don't see any smoke

coming from your house. When my wife bakes, she sets off the fire alarm. It got so bad that the fire department quit coming." He added, "That's because I call them and warn them."

The couple snickered.

With a smile, Ody added, "We're part of the LGBTQ community."

A stern look filled Ivers' face at the revelation. For once, he was speechless.

Ody continued. "I identify as nonbinary myself. Because of my feminine appearance, people often assume that my pronouns are she/her. So, they will usually use those. I'll just gently correct them and say, 'hey, you know what, my pronouns are they/them just FYI, for future reference' or something like that."

"How do you identify?" Dodie asked Ivers.

"Man," was Ivers' one-word response. He was really tiring of the exchange and didn't want to have anything to do with the two wackos.

Ignoring the acerbic tone in Ivers' response, Ody stated softly, "We are so glad to be part of a neighborhood that is so welcoming to the LGBTQ community."

"Whatever you say," Ivers snarled. He was finished with the conversation. "Now why don't you get off my porch before I make a BLT out of you."

"You are too funny," Ody commented quietly. Ody found kindness to win in the long run when confronted with set-in-their-ways people like Ivers.

"Besides, we're vegetarians," Dodie explained.

"Yeah, and I'm Irish," Ivers said as he shut the door. In a second, he reopened it. "Give me those cookies," he said as he snatched the plate of cookies and slammed the door shut.

The two on the porch shrugged their shoulders and began

the short walk home.

Meanwhile, Ivers had walked to the kitchen and set the plate of cookies on the kitchen counter. He decided to save them for dessert that evening even though his stomach was rumbling. He threw a couple of strawberry Pop Tarts in the toaster and made a cup of coffee. It was a late breakfast.

CHAPTER 9

Thursday Afternoon

Ivers had been puttering around on the patio when he heard the front doorbell ring. Immediately his face contorted in a huge frown. It was probably the two aliens from down the street returning, he thought. He walked into the house and grabbed the Super Soaker on his way to the front door.

Before opening the door, he leveled the Super Soaker at his waist with one hand on the trigger, while the other hand reached for the doorknob. He twisted it and threw open the door.

"Don't shoot us, George. For crying out loud, you could hurt someone with that! One blast in the eye and they're blind," Jack Bishop exclaimed as he stepped back.

As Ivers lowered his weapon, he saw that Hudson was standing next to Jack. He let out a deep sigh at the thought of being interrupted. He just wanted to be left alone.

"What do you want?" he groused.

"Phyllis and I were worried that you were okay after being in that rainstorm last night. She wanted me to come over and make sure you were okay," Jack spoke with sincere concern.

"Me, too, Mr. Ivers," Hudson piped up.

"I'm just fine. You can go home now," Ivers directed as he began to shut the door.

"Your wife was worried about you, too," Jack added.

"Charlotte? How did she know about last night?" Ivers asked as he paused shutting the door.

"Phyllis called her," Jack explained. "You know how our wives like to talk," Jack smiled with a wink.

"Yeah. Too much," Ivers retorted.

"Hey George, did you meet the new neighbors who moved in on the other side of us?"

"You mean the Green Arrow and its, they, them or her sidekick?" Ivers snapped.

Jack chuckled. "I guess you did. Did they leave you any cookies?"

"Yes." Ivers was tiring of the conversation.

"Phyllis said that you shouldn't eat them. You don't know what they might have put in them. She's real particular about what she eats."

"I threw them in the trash," Ivers lied. "I gotta go. Tell Phyllis that she can tell my wife that I'm just fine."

"Oh. Okay. I can do that. George, would you like to go over to the senior center tonight with Phyllis and me? We might be going there later."

"Not me. I don't want to go anywhere near that place. Them casserole cougars would be all over me if I went without Charlotte," Ivers muttered.

"Tonight's bingo night," Jack added.

"Not my glass of sweet tea!" Ivers fussed.

"Okay. That's your choice," Jack said. "By the way, Phyllis didn't appreciate you having Hudson put that dead mouse in the microwave. It stunk up the whole house. She had all the windows opened and was spraying air freshener all around," Jack explained seriously.

Ivers was snickering as he listened.

"Yeah, Mr. Ivers. You got me in trouble. My grandmother was really mad, but I told her that it was your idea," Hudson interjected with a frown on his face.

"Did she put you in time out?" Ivers asked hopefully.

"Nah, she didn't really blame me. But she said she's giving

your wife a piece of her mind. How do you do that, Mr. Ivers? Do you have to use a knife?" Hudson asked with a lack of comprehension.

Jack cut off Ivers' response. "I'll explain it to you, Hudson." He didn't want to chance a wild explanation from Ivers.

Jack began to step away when he stopped and called, "You take care, polar bear!" With a giggle, Jack walked away with Hudson in tow.

Ivers shut the door and placed the Super Soaker on the stand by the door just in case the two goofballs from down the street returned. He walked back to the kitchen and poured a glass of sweet tea when the doorbell rang again.

He made his way to the front of the house and peered through the living room window. He saw Hudson had returned and was standing on the porch. With a grimace, Ivers returned to the kitchen while the youngster rang the doorbell several more times.

In a few minutes, Ivers was seated on a patio chair, enjoying his sweet tea. He next heard a squeak from the gate to the back yard. Within seconds, he saw Hudson walk around the garage and approach him on the patio.

"Hey Mr. Ivers, didn't you hear me ringing your doorbell?"

"No," Ivers grumbled.

"Maybe you should get your hearing checked." With a grin, Hudson said, "Knock, knock."

Ivers grimaced. He was in no mood for this silly banter. He didn't answer.

"Knock, knock. Come on Mr. Ivers. You have to say, 'who's there?'" Hudson pleaded.

"Who's there?" Ivers asked stoically.

"Figs."

"Figs who?"

"Figs the doorbell, it's not working!" Hudson roared.

Ivers rolled his eyes and remained silent.

"My grandpa said you belong in a home."

"Your grandpa said that?"

"Yes, and I don't know what he means because you already have a home."

Ivers replied with a frown. "And he said you're going to get a lump of coal in your Christmas stocking." Hudson wandered over to the sliding patio door and peered inside.

"I don't see your Christmas stocking. I don't see a Christmas tree either. Do you have a Christmas tree, Mr. Ivers? Are you going to put it up?" The youngster peppered Ivers with questions.

That's when Ivers remembered that his wife had instructed him to put up the Christmas tree. He had better get that put up before his wife returned home tomorrow, he thought. He decided to ignore the boy and picked up a copy of the State Port Pilot newspaper. He allowed a scowl to cross his face, hoping Hudson would go home.

Meanwhile, Hudson looked into the backyard and noticed the old, unused clothesline. With a puzzled look, he turned to Ivers. "Mr. Ivers, why do you have those two lines of rope tied between those two posts in your backyard?"

Grimacing, Ivers peered over his glasses at the youngster. He didn't like being interrupted. "That's my tightrope. I use it for acrobatics," he replied in an acerbic tone as he returned to his newspaper.

"Really?" the wide-eyed boy asked. He stood and began dragging a chair toward one of the posts.

As the chair squeaked on the patio floor, Ivers looked up.

"What are you doing?" he grumbled.

"I'm going to try walking the tightrope. I saw it done at the circus once," the determined Hudson responded.

"No. No. Don't do that. That's a clothesline," Ivers grunted, angry at the disruption to his reading.

"What's a clothesline?" Hudson asked as he stopped and turned to Ivers.

"You hang your clothes on it to dry in the sun," Ivers snapped. "And," Ivers added with a sly grin, "it's the best way to scare away those pesky squirrels. They can't stand the sight of my polka-dot undershorts flapping in the wind!"

Hudson burst into giggles, picturing the squirrels fleeing in terror from Ivers' fearsome undergarments.

"Are you going to use it today? I don't think I ever saw a clothesline being used."

"No. We don't use it anymore."

"Why?"

"We have a clothes dryer in the house."

"Oh."

Ivers saw a chance to prank the boy. "Another reason we don't use the clothesline is because every time Mrs. Ivers hung the clothes, the squirrels turned her underpants into a trampoline. They were doing all kinds of flips on them!"

Picturing squirrels doing acrobatics, Hudson burst into laughter.

"And that's not all," Ivers continued, warming up to his tale. "The squirrels even used my T-shirts as parachutes. Then there were the birds. They thought my socks were the start of a fancy new nest collection. I found twigs and leaves in them for weeks!"

Hudson snorted, trying to hold back more laughter.

Ivers was on a roll. "Oh, and let's not forget Mrs. Ivers' cat. It thought the clothesline was its personal tightrope. Gave me quite a show, that one did, until it slipped through the leg of a pair of my boxers and fell to the ground."

"Did it get hurt?" Hudson asked with concern.

"Nah. It just ran away." Ivers leaned toward Hudson. "That clothesline has become my personal entertainment center."

"Why?" Hudson asked eagerly.

Before Ivers began to explain, he noticed a movement out of the corner of his eyes. Two squirrels had returned to the clothesline and were playing tag, scampering and leaping from line to line as they chittered. Ivers wasn't the only one to notice. The squirrels had captured Snookums' attention.

"Look at the clothesline."

"There's two squirrels," Hudson exclaimed excitedly.

"Be quiet and watch what the cat does," Ivers whispered softly.

As the squirrels zipped along the clothesline, Snookums watched with growing indignation. Stealthily, it crept towards the clothesline, its every step silent and calculated. The squirrels, too engrossed in their game of tag, remained blissfully unaware of the approaching predator.

With a flick of its tail, it launched itself into the fray, paws outstretched and eyes wide with determination. The chase was on as the cat quickly climbed the wooden post! The squirrels, chittering with glee, darted and dodged with daring leaps.

Snookums bounded after them, a streak of fur and fury, but every time it thought it had them cornered, they'd pull off a spectacular escape. It leaped with all its might, but instead of landing on the squirrels, it found itself clinging to the clothesline, swinging back and forth like a feline trapeze artist.

Finally, with a less-than-graceful dismount, Snookums landed on the soft grass and glared at the two squirrels. Sensing the game was nearing its end, they made a break for the safety of their tree where they continued their chittering. Meanwhile, Snookums sauntered to a sunny spot in the yard, quite pleased with itself for chasing the squirrels from its domain.

"That was funny," Hudson exclaimed. "I bet you have a lot of fun watching those squirrels and your cat."

"They're nothing more than a bunch of trouble," Ivers harrumphed. He decided to spin one more tale to the youngster. "You need to ask your grandpa about the day my hat flew off the clothesline."

"Okay. What happened?" the boy smiled in anticipation of another wild story that he could ask his grandpa about.

"Yep. It was a windy day, and my hat flew over the fence and landed on your grandpa's barbecue."

"How do you know it landed on his barbecue?" Hudson asked skeptically.

"Because your grandpa yelled over the fence."

"Did it catch on fire?"

"No. Your grandpa asked if I'd like my hat back after he snatched it off the grill. I told him to toss it back medium-rare!" Ivers explained as he cracked a rare smile.

Ivers was tiring of the exchange. Slowly he stood from his chair. "You stay here. I'll be right back."

Ivers walked into the garage and returned in a few minutes. He was carrying a small bag in his hand and had a plan for getting Hudson to go back to his grandparents' house.

"Hudson, if you can tell me what the capital of Romania is, I'll give you the surprise that's in this bag."

"A surprise! What is it? Can I see it?" Hudson asked, excited at receiving a gift. He bounded over to Ivers and reached for the bag.

"No. You have to tell me what the capital of Romania is," Ivers demanded firmly.

Hudson wrinkled his brow, and he thought really hard. After a minute, he asked, "Can you give me a clue? What's the first letter?"

"R," Ivers said with a sly grin.

"R. R," Hudson repeated as he concentrated. "I know. It's Rome! I've heard about the Romans. They live in Romania, don't they," he beamed at his knowledge level.

"Oh my! What a smart boy you are!" Ivers relished tricking the youngster.

"Can I have the surprise now?" Hudson asked as he reached for the bag.

Ivers handed him the bag and watched as the boy opened it. Hudson's smile disappeared, replaced by a quizzical look.

"Seeds?" he asked with disappointment.

"These aren't ordinary seeds, Hudson. They are very special."

"What's so special about them, Mr. Ivers?"

"These are bird seeds. I'm going to give you these bird seeds to take home and plant," Ivers said in a very serious tone, although he worked hard at holding back a laugh.

"Plant?"

"Yes. You plant these seeds, and you'll grow birds," Ivers continued in that serious tone.

"What kind of birds?"

"It's a surprise. You might get a bluebird or even an eagle."

"Really?" The boy was wide-eyed with excitement.

"Sometimes you could get an ostrich although you might

have to pull its head out of the ground," Ivers advised somberly.

Hudson squinted his eyes as he conjured up the image of an ostrich with its head buried. "Yeah. I get it. I've read about them burying their head in the ground. I didn't know it was when they were born," he said with an expression of newfound knowledge.

"Why don't you run along to your grandparents' house now and show them?" Ivers suggested, wanting to get rid of the little disruption to his quiet afternoon.

"Okay," Hudson said as he walked quickly around the attached garage, carrying the treasure bag of bird seed. The gate swung shut behind him with a loud clang.

Ivers wandered into the garage and emerged a few minutes later. In his hand, he had a padlock which he placed on the gate. That would keep the little urchin from bothering him, he smiled as he returned to the patio.

He stopped suddenly when he saw the cat. It was sitting in his chair. "Go on! Be off with you!" he yelled as Snookums ran across the patio, disappearing through the cat door. A minute later, it was staring at Ivers from inside the house through the glass patio door.

Remembering again that he needed to set up the Christmas tree, Ivers entered the house. Seeing the plate of cookies, he paused to examine them. Holding one up, he inspected it closely. It looked fine, he thought as he cautiously took a bite. It tasted better than it looked, he thought as he gobbled it down. He ate a second one before washing it down with a small glass of milk. He decided to wash the dishes in the kitchen sink before going downstairs to get the Christmas tree.

A few minutes later, Ivers noticed that the water from the kitchen faucet became colorful. He thought for a moment that the white plates and bowls in the dish rack also had taken on colorful hues. He then noticed the silverware in the dish drainer had started dancing, and the kitchen walls seemed to breathe. Shaking his head from side to side, he tried to clear his mind. He felt light-headed, and strange things seemed to be happening.

He gripped the edge of the counter tightly when he saw shadows dancing along the walls. It seemed like the room was getting warmer. He thought he heard music playing, and it sounded quite good, like a whimsical symphony. That meant it wasn't coming from Jack next door.

Confused, Ivers made his way to one of the kitchen chairs and sat down as the room seemed to whirl around him like a mad carousel. The kitchen was transforming before his eyes while the cookies laced with magic mushroom powder caused hallucinations. The kitchen clock hands raced around as if trying to win a marathon.

Ivers looked down at his white beard and saw that several cookie crumbs had fallen onto it. They appeared to be moving like little ants, and his beard seemed to be growing longer in front of his eyes.

The floor tiles underfoot morphed into a wavy ocean. He also found himself floating, his chair now a vessel navigating his kitchen coastline. As the magic mushroom potency peaked, the old man listened to the refrigerator, humming a deep bass while the oven mitts clapped along.

Eventually, the enchantment began to wane, and the magical experience gently faded. The old man uttered a satisfied sigh and drifted off to sleep for 30 minutes. When he awoke, he again shook his head. He was still a bit woozy from the effects of the cookies. Carefully, he stood and looked around. Everything had nearly returned to normal.

Still feeling the lingering effects from the cookies, he stumbled across the room to the basement door. He needed to get that Christmas tree. Swinging open the door, he contemplated going downstairs as the cat watched from under the kitchen table.

His wife earlier had hung the garland and wreath on the front of the house. She knew where everything was in that basement. Why couldn't she have brought up that artificial Christmas tree, he pondered silently during a brief moment of clarity.

Ivers stared down the creaky stairs into the dank abyss as he contemplated a daring descent into its dark labyrinth. He hated going into the basement. It was filled with too many memories and relics from the past – memories that haunted him at night.

Switching on the bare lightbulb at the bottom of the stairs, he began his descent to the accompaniment of groans. The groans emitted not just from the wooden steps, but also from his knees. The air was thick with dust and a musty smell. Rays of light tried to illuminate the basement as they pierced through several small openings in the concrete, mold-covered block walls.

When he finally took the last step, Ivers stopped and looked around. It was silent. Standing still, his knees no longer sounded like a bowl of Rice Krispies. He surveyed his surroundings. The cobwebs draped over dust-covered boxes. A mouse scurried across the floor in front of him, its tiny feet pattering like raindrops on a tin roof.

Carefully making his way to the middle of the cluttered basement, Ivers reached up, trying to find the pull string for the overhead light. After several attempts, his fingers grasped it and pulled. The 25-watt bulb did very little to chase away the eerie darkness. Ivers now wished that he had used a brighter bulb.

He began rummaging through the boxes, finding artifacts of

his past life. He didn't spend much time there as he wanted to find the Christmas tree and return upstairs. He was very careful to avoid the boxes in the far corner of the basement. He didn't need any reminder of the memories they contained. He wanted his wife to get rid of them, but she wouldn't relent to his wishes.

He spotted the artificial tree perched precariously atop a dusty shelf. It was out of his reach. He looked around the dimly lit room and saw a stool. He grabbed it and set it in front of the shelving unit. Stepping on it carefully, he discovered that it was wobbly and worn. Grasping the shelf unit with one hand, he took another step cautiously as the stool threatened to break.

As his fingers grazed the tree, the stool tottered. Ivers teetered in a ballet of flailing limbs and startled exclamations. Unable to maintain his balance while fighting the law of gravity, Ivers tumbled to a mercilessly hard floor.

The old man lay injured on the cold concrete floor - a tangle of limbs and pride. However, there was one problem. When his head hit the floor, he incurred a nasty bump on his bald head and began to bleed. He passed out.

An hour later, Ivers slowly stirred back to consciousness, his mind a foggy haze. With a groan that seemed to echo off the concrete walls, he blinked open his eyes. His surroundings seemed murky, and his head throbbed from its contact with the unforgiving floor. He lay there for a moment, gathering his wits, as memories of the fall trickled back into his mind like unwelcome guests.

As he tried to clear the fog from his mind, he noticed the appearance of a gentle apparition above him. He slowly shook his head to clear the cobwebs. What was he seeing, he wondered. Squinting his eyes despite the pain in his head, he saw a forgiving specter, the visage of his late son. The old man's eyes brimmed with unshed tears.

"Son, is that you?" he asked in disbelief.

"Yes, Dad. It's me," the apparition whispered like the rustling of leaves.

The old man's voice trembled as he spoke, "Georgie, I've missed you so much. My heart has been heavy with regret."

"Why? It wasn't your fault."

"If I hadn't called out to you while you were in the crosswalk, you wouldn't have turned around to look at me. You would have seen the car crashing the red traffic light. The one that struck you and took you away from us," Ivers murmured, his voice a soft echo of love and longing.

"Dad, I'm at peace, and my desire is that you're at peace," his son said quietly.

"Forgive me, Son," Ivers pleaded in a loving tone.

"Dad, you don't need to ask for my forgiveness. You need to forgive yourself. That's the burden that you are carrying," his son explained.

The old man listened, his heart swelling with a love that endured beyond death's door. His son's words of love and forgiveness embraced Ivers' soul.

"We can't go back in time, but we can rewind the warm memories in our mind. And forgive yourself just as Christ forgave us."

As the apparition began to fade, he spoke, "We'll meet again, but you need to forgive yourself and be the dad I was so proud of and loved so much."

"Don't go!" Ivers begged as the apparition vanished, leaving the old man in a serene solace. With his eyes lifted towards the heavens, Ivers slipped back into a state of unconsciousness.

An hour later, Snookums realized that it hadn't seen Mr.

Grumpy in some time. With a flick of its tail, it emerged from under the kitchen table where it had napped and began its search. It peered through the patio door to see if he was in the back yard but couldn't spot him. It then scanned the kitchen area and roamed throughout the house but to no avail. The house was devoid of human presence as there were no apparent signs of the crusty curmudgeon.

Seeing the open basement door, the cat speculated with a twitch of its whiskers that he may have gone downstairs. The cat moved to the top of the stairs and stared into the creepy basement. With each passing moment, the cat's curiosity grew.

As Snookums descended the creaky wooden stairs to the basement, its keen feline senses detected something amiss. There, amidst the shadows lay Ivers, motionless on the cold concrete floor. Snookums, though mostly at odds with the old man, knew this was no time for it to be aloof.

The cat approached Ivers and circled his body as it looked for signs of life. It saw his chest rising and falling as well as blood on the floor. Snookums pawed at his hand to see if he'd react. Getting no response, the cat jumped on Ivers' chest, but still no reaction.

With the agility of a seasoned acrobat, the cat leaped onto a nearby shelf, knocking over a jar of bolts that clattered and echoed through the basement. It positioned itself next to the basement window and began to meow as loudly as it could.

Ten minutes later, Hudson appeared at the basement window. "What's wrong, Snookums?" he asked as he tried to peer through the dirty window at the cat on the other side. The cat continued its loud meows.

Hudson lay on his stomach and scrunched his face against the glass. That's when he saw Ivers on the floor.

"Hey Mr. Ivers, are you okay?" he yelled.

There was no response from the motionless Ivers.

"Mr. Ivers, are you okay?" Hudson shouted again through the glass window.

Not getting any response to his shouts, Hudson told the cat, "Snookums, you stay right there. I'll get my grandpa and grandma. They'll know what to do."

Hudson popped to his feet and ran next door. Entering the kitchen, he found his grandparents talking. "You've got to help Mr. Ivers," he spoke breathlessly. "I think he's dead," the boy exclaimed seriously.

"Slow down, cowboy," Jack countered. "What's going on with George?"

"I heard Snookums meowing when I was playing in the side yard. So, I went over, and the cat was standing just inside the basement window. When I looked in the window, I saw Mr. Ivers. He's dead on the basement floor."

"Phyllis, you better call 911," Jack said as he started out of the house.

"I'll get them on the phone. You go ahead. I'll be right over," Phyllis said urgently as she feared the worst.

"You come with me," Jack said to Hudson as the two raced out of the house and next door.

Hudson led him to the basement window where the cat was still meowing. "Look in there," Hudson pointed.

Jack dropped to his knees and peered through the window. He could see Ivers on the floor. "George. George," Jack called loudly. "Are you okay?"

Getting no response, Jack led Hudson to the front of the house. When he spotted the bedroom window partially open and the torn screen on the ground, he instructed Hudson. "Come over here. I'm going to open this window more and boost you up. You go through the open window and walk around to the front door to open it. Understand?"

"Yes."

In less than a minute, Hudson opened the front door for Jack and Phyllis, who had joined him.

"You stay here and wait for the rescue squad. Then you bring them downstairs, Hudson," Phyllis directed.

"Okay Grandma," Hudson replied.

Jack and Phyllis moved quickly through the house and descended the stairs.

"George needs better lighting down here," Jack observed as they reached the bottom of the steps.

"I'll say. This basement gives me the willies," she added. Suddenly she screamed.

"What's wrong Phyllis?" Jack asked, stopping in his tracks.

"Something just rubbed against my legs." She looked down and saw Snookums weaving between her legs in a figure-eight pattern. "Oh Jack, it's the cat."

Seeing that it had their attention, the cat led them to Ivers' still body. Kneeling next to Ivers as the cat sat on its haunches, Jack called, "George, are you okay."

"Jack, look at the blood on the floor," Phyllis said in a panicked voice.

"I see it, Phyllis."

"Is he breathing?" Phyllis pushed.

Jack placed his hand on Ivers' chest. "Yes." Jack leaned closer to Ivers. "George. Wake up, George."

With a moan, Ivers' eyes fluttered open from his unintended slumber.

"Are you okay?" Jack asked again.

"I fell," Ivers explained as he tried to prop himself up on shaky elbows. "Help me get up."

"You shouldn't do that George. You're bleeding and the rescue squad will be here in a couple of minutes," Phyllis said nervously as they heard the rescue squad park in front of the house.

With a groan and Jack's assistance, Ivers barely lifted himself to a sitting position. He saw the blood on the floor and touched his head. When he brought his hand back to his eyes, he saw the blood on it.

"I'll be fine. Just help me to my feet and I'll wash it off," Ivers said stubbornly.

"You're not doing anything of that kind. You're staying put," Phyllis instructed firmly as the sound of running feet overhead announced the arrival of the paramedics in the house. Within seconds they descended the stairs and approached Ivers.

Seeing the overturned stool and the blood on Ivers' head, the first paramedic asked, "Take a bad fall, sir?"

"Yes, but I'll be fine. I don't need to bother anyone."

"No bother," the paramedic said as he and his partner began taking vitals.

Twenty minutes later, Ivers was being wheeled into the back of the ambulance. Its doors were wide open like the arms of a caring mother.

"Don't call my wife, Phyllis," he shouted as the door closed.

"I'm calling her right now," Phyllis said as she, Jack and Hudson returned home.

One of the paramedics closed the ambulance doors, ending any further exchange between Ivers and the Bishops. With its sirens wailing, it left for the emergency room as a number of neighbors watched from their porches.

"We're going to drive over to the hospital and make sure

he's okay," Jack said as he led Phyllis and Hudson toward his car.

"Can I come, too?" Hudson asked eagerly.

"Of course, you can, Hudson. You're a hero," Jack said proudly.

"A superhero!" Phyllis interjected.

"And so is Snookums," Hudson beamed.

"That's right," Jack agreed.

When the ambulance arrived at the hospital emergency room entrance, Ivers was whisked inside where he went through a number of examinations and tests. Two hours later, Ivers was wheeled into a private room where he was being kept overnight for observation, much to his chagrin. Sporting a large bandage on his head, Ivers was fully awake and resting in his bed when Jack, Phyllis and Hudson walked into his room.

"How are you feeling, George?" Jack probed with concern as he looked at his bedridden neighbor.

"I'm doing fine. They should let me go home," he muttered.

"You just rest. The doctor said you may be released tomorrow, and Charlotte will be home tomorrow," Phyllis explained.

"You called her?" Ivers asked.

"Yes, I did. She has a right to know, George," Phyllis retorted seriously.

Ivers reacted with a grimace, then asked, "What made you come looking for me?"

Jack explained how the meowing cat attracted Hudson's attention which led to them entering the house and finding him on the basement floor.

"Snookums reported my fall and injury?" Ivers asked in amazement. He couldn't believe the cat would go to bat for him after the way he mistreated it.

"Yes. Snookums and Hudson worked as a team," Jack said proudly as he beamed at his grandson.

Ivers turned to Hudson. "Thank you for being a hero," he said gratefully.

"My grandma said I was a superhero," Hudson proudly corrected Ivers.

"Well, that's what it is then. You're a superhero." For the first time in a long time, Ivers allowed them to see a smile creep onto his face.

"And so is Snookums!" Hudson piped up.

Ivers nodded his head in agreement.

"George, we're going to let you get your rest. I'll be over in the morning to bring you home," Jack said as the three of them started for the door. "Toodle-loo, kangaroo!"

"Thank you," Ivers called after them.

As they walked down the hall, Phyllis turned to Jack. "Did I just see a smile on George's face and hear him say thank you?"

"I believe so," Jack answered.

"He needs to get boinked on the head more often. Probably knocked some sense into him," Phyllis stated firmly.

"That reminds me of a knock-knock joke," Hudson interrupted as they continued walking down the hall.

Meanwhile, Ivers was replaying the afternoon's events in his mind and the revelation that the Bishops had provided him about his rescue. What a critical role that four-legged furry pet played in coming to his aid even though he had mistreated it. After all, it's not every day a cat gets to save their human from the perils of the basement floor.

The fall had been a jarring reminder of his mortality and a blessing in disguise. He thought back to the visionary encounter with his son. Was it real or had he dreamed it? He wasn't sure.

As he stared at the ceiling of his hospital room with the beeping of machines in the background, Ivers began a journey of introspection. He wrestled with the weight of regret he had carried since the death of his son. It was like a suitcase filled with anger and past grievances - one that needed to be unpacked and freed. Life was too fragile to be carrying that luggage.

An epiphany struck him about the encounter with his son – real or not. He had been so buried in despair and unforgiveness at the thought of causing his son's death. It had haunted him for the last several years. So much so that he had truly placed real life on pause. It was time to hit the play button and start living again.

He hadn't been to church in years despite the pleas from his wife. Ivers now felt a need to pray. He bowed his head in silent prayer for several minutes as he asked for forgiveness and forgave himself.

When he opened his eyes, he felt like a burden had been lifted from his shoulders as he went through a profound transformation. With a newfound zest, he vowed to fill the remaining chapters of his life with laughter, love, and a dash of reckless abandon.

As he lay there with a gentle smile of reconciliation, he knew that he was no longer a prisoner of the past. He had a second chance and needed to make the most of it. He began planning the changes that he would make in his relationships with others, how he would be more tolerant, understanding and caring – and especially forgiving.

He took a deep breath and allowed a huge smile to fill his face. He couldn't wait for the next morning for Jack to pick him up and return him home. Charlotte was in for a big surprise – and so was Snookums.

As the bedside table lamp cast a golden glow on his face, Ivers closed his eyes, content that he had made peace with himself. Ready to greet the next day with a positive approach, he fell into a deep slumber. It was the best sleep that he had in years.

CHAPTER 10

Late Friday Morning

"Good morning, George," Jack greeted Ivers as he walked around his parked car outside of the patient discharge area.

Ivers responded with a cheery, "Well if it isn't my friendly neighbor, Jumping Jack Flash! I'm ready to dash, Flash!"

Jack stopped midstep and stared at Ivers, then at the nurse who was standing behind Ivers' wheelchair. "Excuse me. Could you check your patient's wristband and make sure it reads 'George Ivers'? This guy doesn't sound like the George Ivers I know," Jack said with mock concern.

"Oh, we already checked," the nurse replied. "From what I heard about a cranky patient arriving last night in the emergency room, he's changed to a smiling and happy patient today." She patted Ivers on the shoulder. "Isn't that right, Mr. Ivers?"

"It's a new day, I'm happy to say. No more Mr. Cranky Pants," Ivers smiled as he looked up at the nurse.

Jack had a stunned look on his face. "You better give me a bottle of whatever prescription of nice pills you gave him in case it wears off."

"We didn't give him anything. He was just here for observation, and he passed with better than flying colors," the nurse grinned as she wheeled Ivers to the passenger door which Jack had opened.

"That's incredible," Jack said as he helped Ivers step into the car.

Halfway in the car, Ivers stopped and looked at Jack. "Jack, I have made a big decision."

"You have?"

"Yes. I'm going to be like a pineapple," Ivers said with a twinkle in his eyes.

Frowning as he imagined a pineapple, Jack countered, "All prickly on the outside? I thought you were changing."

"I am, Jack. I'm going to be like a pineapple: standing tall, wearing a crown, and being sweet on the inside," Ivers smiled.

Uttering a deep sigh of relief, Jack retorted, "You had me worried for a second. I thought the old George was coming back."

"Not going to happen, Jack," Ivers said as he settled into the passenger seat. Turning to the nurse, who was about to wheel away the wheelchair, Ivers commented, "Thank you, honey. I hope you have a wonderful day."

"You, too." The nurse smiled and disappeared inside.

Jack walked around the car with a look of disbelief. Was this really going to be the new George, he wondered as he slid into the driver's seat.

As he started the car, Ivers asked, "Do you mind if we stop at the pet store and a couple of other places on the way home?"

"Pet store? I thought I'd never hear you want anything to do with a pet store," Jack countered as the car drove away from the hospital.

Ivers chuckled. "I do have a superhero cat at home who deserves a few treats."

Ivers, who was once a grumpy octogenarian, now was on a new mission of kindness. He wanted to show people that it was never too late to change the narrative of one's life.

An hour later, Jack pulled into Ivers' driveway and parked the car. The two men exited the car and carried numerous bags up to the front porch where Ivers paused.

"Thank you for your help, Jack. I can take these inside."

"Oh no. I'll be glad to help you," he said as he reached for the front doorknob.

"You'll need a key. It always locks when it shuts," Ivers said as he fumbled in his pocket for his house key.

"Not anymore, George. I fixed it for you this morning," Jack stated proudly.

"You did?" Ivers stammered with surprise.

"Yes. That's what neighbors do. They help each other, George. I also replaced the screen on your front bedroom window this morning."

"That was mighty kind of you."

"That's nothing. Wait until you see inside,"

Ivers' face contorted as he tried to determine what Jack had been up to.

Jack swung open the door and the two men walked inside carrying bags that seem to be murmuring with the secrets of a festive feast.

Ivers' jaw dropped when he saw that the front room had been decorated with Christmas decorations, and a brightly lit Christmas tree was in the corner.

"Surprise!" two voices spoke in unison.

Ivers peered around the corner and saw Phyllis and Hudson. Their faces glowed from their morning accomplishment.

"You did this?" Ivers asked, astonished.

"Thought we'd give you a big surprise," Phyllis commented graciously.

"That you did," Ivers said with a look of bewilderment. "I don't know how to thank you. I'm over the moon, June."

"Thank you is just fine. Besides, we knew that Charlotte was coming home late this afternoon and we wanted to help out while you were in the hospital," she added.

"I put the angel on top of the Christmas tree," Hudson piped up, wanting to be recognized.

"And just look how perfectly straight it is," Ivers said as he gazed at the treetop. "You did a wonderful job."

Hudson's face shined with pride. "Do you want to help me set up the manger?"

"I guess I could do that." He set his bags on the sofa and walked to the tree. Slowing dropping to his knees, he helped Hudson set up the manger scene.

Almost finished, Hudson handed Ivers the final piece. "Here's the baby Jesus. You can put him in the manger."

Ivers took the baby Jesus in his hand. As he paused to examine the figure, he remembered years ago when he was on that same floor with his son as a little boy.

His son always had the privilege of placing the baby Jesus in the manger. With a soft smile, he turned to Hudson. "Why don't you take the honor of placing the most important person where He belongs."

"Thank you!" Hudson gleamed as he took the piece from Ivers and set Him in the manager.

While watching the boy, Ivers momentarily contemplated on the significance of Jesus' birth and the forgiveness he brought to the world.

"We should get these bags in the kitchen," Jack offered, interrupting Ivers' thoughts.

"Right." Ivers slowly stood and picked up his bags. He then followed Jack into the kitchen, and they placed the bags on the counter.

"Hudson and I are going home," Phyllis called as the two of them walked out the front door.

"Thank you again," Ivers shouted.

"Think you've got everything you need now?" Jack asked.

"Yes, I do. Thank you. Thank you," Ivers said as he shook Jack's hand.

"You've got enough here for a party," Jack commented as he looked at the food-filled bags on the counter.

"That I do," Ivers said with a hint of mystery.

"Make it a BYOT party," Jack suggested whimsically.

"What?" Ivers asked, not comprehending what Jack meant.

"Bring Your Own Teeth!" Jack chuckled as he walked down the hall. Pausing at the door, Jack shouted, with a grin, one of his trademark farewells. "Till then, penguin!" With a giggle he walked outside, closing the door behind him.

He really had some nice, well-intentioned neighbors, Ivers thought for a moment. He turned his attention to the bags bursting with an assortment of festive treats and gastronomic delights including eggnog, candied nuts, a fruitcake, spiced gingerbread cookies in the shape of reindeer and stars, and a Christmas ham.

Ivers emptied all of the bags but one. Finished, he opened the last bag and began withdrawing the contents. There were several cat toys, including some filled with catnip, and two containers of Snookums' favorite cat treats.

Opening one of the containers, Ivers poured several of the treats in his hand. He then began calling in a soft voice, "Snookums? Snookums? Where are you?"

From under the safe sanctuary of a kitchen chair, Snookums awoke from its nap. It stretched its paws, flicked its tail, and yawned widely, showing off its sharp teeth and pink tongue.

"Snookums, where are you?" Ivers called again.

The cat's whiskers twitched with curiosity. Always an astute observer, Snookums noticed the softness in the man's voice with a mix of suspicion and intrigue. It knew that he had never been much of a cat person, often tricking the cat with a promise of treats that were swapped out with a whack from a folded newspaper.

The cat wondered with skepticism if a transformation was taking place. It was more used to the man finding ways to douse it in water or slam the patio door in its face when it tried to run inside. Could it really trust the usually stern-voiced Ivers who was now cooing and offering it a treat? Was it being set up again?

Ivers spotted the cat under the chair and slowly dropped to his knees, something that the cat had never seen before. "I have treats for you, Snookums. You deserve them. I just can't believe that you are responsible for rescuing me," Ivers added as he held out a peace offering to the four-legged feline.

The cat was still wary and didn't budge, which caused Ivers to drop the treats on the floor and push them toward the cat.

"I know that you don't believe that I'm trying to be nice to you. I've changed. I want you and me to be friends," Ivers explained, inching the treats closer to the cat.

Snookums, with its eyes narrowing to slits of disapproval, was unimpressed. The treats were tempting, but the cat was suspicious that it may be a trick as was its experience in the past with this human. It waited and watched, unmoving except for an occasional tail flick. It didn't want to lose the upper paw during this encounter.

Trying a different tactic, Ivers left the treats on the floor and slowly stood on his creaky knees. "I'll leave you alone. I know it will take some time to win your confidence, but I really do want to start over again, my feline friend. Let's have a fresh start."

The words triggered a memory. He had purchased a bag of

Fresh Start kitty litter and needed to change it before his wife returned. Picking up a catnip-filled toy mouse from the table, he dropped it on the floor. "You can enjoy the catnip and the treats while I change your litter," Ivers said as he left to do the chore that he had once hated.

Ivers walked to the corner of the kitchen where the litter box was placed. With a deep sigh that echoed through the kitchen, he reached for the bright yellow scoop and bent down. He scooped up the clumps of litter and dumped them in the nearby bucket. Finished, he took the bucket outside and dumped it into the garbage can.

From across the room, the cat watched with disbelieving eyes. It eased itself out from under the kitchen chair and began devouring the treats. It next began to play with the catnip-filled mouse, rolling it around and pulling it in close with its paws as it purred loudly.

Returning from the garage, Ivers grabbed the bag of fresh kitty litter. He opened it and began pouring it into the box. He then set the bag down and turned his attention to the cat that had clawed its way into his heart.

When he washed his hands at the kitchen sink, the cat walked over to inspect the litter box. Satisfied with the cleanliness of its realm, the cat offered a solitary purr of approval. Setting its misgivings aside, the cat began to succumb to Ivers' newfound affection as it rubbed against Ivers' ankles – surprising him.

Ivers surprised himself, too, when he reached down and scratched the cat below its ears, receiving a louder purr.

"I'm so sorry for how I treated you," he said quietly. The cat sat on its hindquarters and looked up expectantly at Ivers. "Pick me up," the cat seemed to be saying to Ivers.

With a changed heart and a creak in his knees, Ivers bent down and scooped up the cat he had so recently hated. He cradled the feline with a newfound gentleness and began stroking its soft fur.

"I might not be here today if it weren't for you. I heard about what you did from the Bishops and Hudson. You are such a superhero, aren't you?" Ivers said in an appreciative tone.

Snookums, equally surprised by this turn of events, went limp in his arms, its initial hesitation melting into a purring acquiescence. The cat nuzzled in his chest as Ivers sported a spreading smile. It was the beginning of an unexpected friendship.

Carrying the cat to the front room, Ivers eased himself into his rocker across from the Christmas tree. He was filled with a sense of peace as he beheld the kaleidoscope of festive lights that twinkled on the tree. This year's Christmas had a new meaning for Ivers, who continued stroking the cat.

Snookums was filled with contentment in its newfound relationship with Ivers. As Ivers rubbed its belly, the cat purred as loud as a lion's roar. Ivers had changed, and with him, so had the cat. As the duo rocked, Ivers thought through a plan to surprise his wife when she arrived home late afternoon.

CHAPTER 11

Late Friday Afternoon

With its tires crunching softly on the white limestone driveway, Charlotte parked in front of the garage door and turned off the engine. She was weary from the drive from Raleigh and the visit with her ailing sister, but glad to be home for Christmas Eve – especially after George's fall. She was anxious to see how he was doing even though Phyllis had called her that morning to let her know he was fine.

From the driver's seat, she could see the Christmas tree aglow through the front room window. She smiled with the visible knowledge that George had taken time to put up the Christmas tree. As she studied her welcoming home with its soft lights, she sensed something different in the air. She wasn't sure, but her woman's intuition was telling her that something perhaps had changed.

With a gentle sigh, she stepped out and took a deep breath. The air was crisp, carrying the scent of the ocean and the faintest whisper of the surrounding live oaks. She walked up to the front door that was draped with garland. She reached for her keys and began to insert them in the door when the door swung open unexpectedly.

"Welcome home!"

Charlotte was stunned. "I wasn't expecting you to be here," she commented with surprise.

"Neither did I. Come on in," Phyllis said as she led Charlotte inside.

"There's Christmas music playing?" she queried quizzically. "George doesn't like Christmas music playing," she explained as she noticed the warm scent of cinnamon and pine from several burning candles.

"Ha-ha. It's no problem. George is the one who put it on," Phyllis laughed.

Charlotte paused to gaze at the front room, noting George's cane was leaning against the sofa. He apparently wasn't using it, she thought. "The tree and decorations look wonderful. Better than what you described on the phone earlier."

"They do look nice, don't they? Come on back to the kitchen with me. You're not going to believe this," Phyllis explained, grabbing Charlotte's arm.

"Wait a second. I better go outside and check the address. I'm not sure that I'm in the right house," a confused Charlotte stated.

"Ha ha. You are Charlotte. Wait until you see this," Phyllis urged as she tugged Charlotte along to the kitchen. Laughter was ringing through the house like jingle bells.

When they entered the back of the house, Charlotte found several people in the kitchen and a counter was covered with an array of Christmas cookies and food-laden trays.

"George bought all of the food and cookies. The food trays were delivered about an hour ago," Phyllis stated warmly. "I baked the Christmas ham that George bought. It is so tasty," she added gleefully.

This was extraordinary. George didn't like company, or especially spending money. What was going on, she wondered as she looked around.

"Hi, Charlotte. Join the party," Jill Tracy greeted her with a big holiday hug.

"Party?" Charlotte stammered in disbelief as Jill's husband, Steve, and daughter, Thea, stepped up to also give Charlotte a welcome home hug.

"George is throwing a Christmas party!" Jill explained.

"That's right. You're going to love this," Phyllis added as the wide-eyed Charlotte scanned the room.

Her eyes stopped and focused on two strangers - one had spiked green hair while the other had purple hair that was cut Mohawk-style. "Does George know that those two people are here? You know how he doesn't like that far out stuff!"

"Oh yes. He knows. George walked over to their house and personally invited them. That's Ody and Dodie Raymond. They just moved in on the other side of our house while you were away," Phyllis answered.

Charlotte's mind reeled as she listened. "George did that?"

"Yes, he did."

"He must not be feeling well," Charlotte suggested.

"I think he's at the top of his game, the best I've ever seen from him."

"Incredible. And speaking of George, where is Mr. Wonderful?"

"Over there." Phyllis pointed to the far wall where Ivers was sitting on the floor.

Charlotte caught sight of Ivers, with Snookums nestled in his lap, emitting purrs of pure bliss. Ivers, who had donned a festive Santa hat, beamed as he pampered the feline's coat. It was hard to tell who was purring more contently, George or Snookums.

"Perhaps I should venture out more," Charlotte mused in astonishment. She gazed at her husband, her eyes wide with surprise. The sight of him so engrossed with the cat and exuding such yuletide cheer was unexpected. The Santa hat paired with his snowy beard gave him an uncanny resemblance to Mr. Claus himself.

"He and Snookums have become fast friends. Remember what I told you on the phone? Snookums is responsible for George's rescue from that nasty fall he took. That cat follows him everywhere since this afternoon. That's my grandson, Hudson, next to him by the drums."

Charlotte shook her head with amazement as she heard a jovial Ivers telling Hudson knock-knock jokes. "You know that George doesn't like the noise of drums, right?"

"Are you kidding me? He's the one who suggested Hudson bring his drums over. Not only that, but he asked my Jack to bring his guitar over so we could sing some Christmas carols."

"Sing? George doesn't like to sing," Charlotte exclaimed.

"If you ask me, that boink on his head when he fell did George some real good," Phyllis suggested happily.

"I'll say."

Across the room, Ivers looked up and saw his wife. He waved at her and gently placed the sleeping feline on the floor before standing to his feet. Walking over to her, he wrapped his arms tightly around her.

"Welcome home, honey. I missed you," he said affectionately.

"George, I am so impressed. I love this new you that I've heard so much about," she whispered in his ear.

Smiling, Ivers stepped back so that he could look into his wife's eyes. "And the new me is here to stay."

With a loving countenance on her face, Charlotte asked, "And this is all due to you hitting your head and getting some sense knocked into that thick skull of yours?"

"Let's step out on the patio for a few minutes where we can talk," Ivers suggested as he led her by the hand outside.

Shutting the patio door behind them, he turned to face his wife. "It wasn't my head on the basement floor that caused the change. It was Georgie."

Dumfounded by his revelation, she stared at her husband. He had forbidden the mention of Georgie's name since his traumatic death several years ago. The mention of their son's name would send Ivers spiraling downward into an emotional abyss filled with regret and torturous memories. He had refused counseling and blamed himself for distracting his son in the crosswalk. Otherwise, he'd have seen the vehicle speeding through the red light before it struck and killed him.

"Georgie? What do you mean?" she asked, raising her eyebrow with a touch of skepticism, humor and heartwarming sentiment.

"I saw him, and he talked to me while I was down on the basement floor yesterday."

"Are you sure? Maybe you were just imagining things," she probed with incredulity. Their son had been the apple of Ivers' eye. He deeply loved his son and relished every moment they had together.

"I couldn't be any more positive," Ivers replied in a convincing tone.

"Maybe it was the result of an empty bottle of Merlot," she suggested.

"Charlotte, it wasn't. It was Georgie." Ivers leaned toward her and proceeded to describe the unexpected encounter in vivid detail.

She listened intently as he recounted the words of their son, words only he would know. Her eyes widened, her mouth was ajar, and a shiver ran down her spine. Could it be? With a tremor of hope and her mind churning with memories of their son, a part of her wanted to believe in this ethereal exchange. As her husband then talked about his meditations in the hospital bed, she found herself drawn into the narrative, her heart a pendulum swinging between doubt and yearning.

Upon hearing her husband's declaration of self-forgiveness for their son's death after years weighed down by grief and unforgiveness, her eyes glistened with tears.

"George, I want you to know that my sister and I spent some time in prayer for you while I visited with her. This is a real answer to prayer. Forgiveness is like a gentle tide that washes away the hurtful feelings of regret, leaving behind a smooth sandy beach of contentment," she whispered supportively.

"Contentment. That's something I haven't experienced in years," Ivers said softly as he gently placed an arm around his wife. "I feel like an unbearable burden has been lifted from my shoulders, and from my heart and soul."

Her heart ached with love and compassion for her husband. "We forgive, not because it erases the past, but because it frees us from it." She reached up and caressed the side of his face and his white beard, "Shall we go back inside and join our friends?"

"In a minute," he said as he turned and leaned into his wife to give her a loving kiss. His beard brushed gently against her cheek as they shared a kiss of a deep, abiding love that had weathered the storms of life.

"Thank you for putting up with me, Charlotte," he whispered.

"It hasn't always been easy," she replied with a twinkle in her eyes. "Now, let's go see our friends."

When they reentered the kitchen, Snookums was the first to greet them, rubbing against Ivers' ankles. Ivers bent down and picked up the cat and began stroking its fur.

"Where have you two been?" Phyllis asked with a sly grin.

Before Ivers could reply, Charlotte answered, "Smooching on the patio!"

Ivers' head snapped around in surprise to stare at his wife. He then allowed a smile to cross his face. "We had some catching up to do. Jack, why don't you and Hudson lead us in some Christmas carols since you both are excellent vocalists?"

The next hour was filled with singing carols and munching on the Christmas food as the house filled with the spirit of Christmas and shouts from Ivers of "A blessed Merry Christmas to one and all!"

COMING SOON
Next *Emerson Moore* Adventure:
Breakwater Bay

Other Bob Adamov Novels

#1 Rainbow's End

In 1864, Confederate raiders launched a daring mission from Canada to liberate officers held captive on Johnson's Island. The mystery deepens with the discovery of a corpse on Rattlesnake Island, marking the start of a decades-long hunt for an elusive trunk.

Fast forward to 2001, an investigative reporter, while visiting his aunt in Put-in-Bay, tangles with a powerful shipping tycoon as he delves into the raid's history and the trunk's disappearance. Amidst this, he struggles to manage his intense attraction to a married woman he encounters on South Bass Island. The original edition is out of print and is replaced by the rewritten 20th anniversary edition.

#2 Pierce the Veil

In this gripping novel, Max Ratek, a Wall Street legend known for his corporate takeovers, sets his sights on a tire company based in Cuyahoga Falls, Ohio. However, his covert operation is jeopardized when the company's investor relations expert, grappling with MS and wheelchair-bound, uncovers his plot and decides to counterattack. Meanwhile, Emerson Moore, an investigative reporter in Put-in-Bay, stumbles upon Ratek's nefarious scheme. Thrust into a whirlwind of corporate espionage, Moore navigates through perilous waters, untimely deaths, and explosive events, all while facing a formidable CEO and Ratek's enigmatic blonde associate, known for her icy demeanor.

#3 When Rainbows Walk

In 1622, the Spanish galleon Atocha succumbed to a hurricane near the Marquesas Islands, its $400 million treasure lost until Mel Fisher discovered it centuries later and showcased it in his Key West Museum.

Meanwhile, a desperate terrorist on the run from the Mossad and a mobster in the Federal Witness Protection program form an unlikely alliance, targeting this treasure amidst the eye of Hurricane Charley. Investigative reporter Emerson Moore and his companion, ex-Navy SEAL Sam Duncan, dive into a whirlwind of danger and deceit in Key West. It's a tapestry of treachery and maritime adventure, leading readers through a labyrinth of lethal encounters, underwater escapades and a twist-filled finale.

#4 Promised Land

In the turmoil of the Battle of Trafalgar, a Vatican envoy is assassinated, and a precious gold cross with a cryptic message is taken. This relic reemerges in New Orleans post-Hurricane Katrina. Investigative reporter Emerson Moore is drawn into a web of murder and mystery in Put-in-Bay and the French Quarter, entangled with stolen Vatican documents.

A colorful cast emerges, including a bold Creole detective and her partner "Elmo," a whimsical swamp-dwelling father, a haughty cardiologist, and a troubled priest. "Promised Land" weaves a tale of intrigue from Lake Erie's shores to the French Quarter's heart, blending police corruption, medical drama, deadly wildlife, Hurricane Katrina's aftermath, and chilling murders. Moore's investigation also uncovers a document that questions the legitimacy of the United States as a nation.

#5 The Other Side of Hell

In the midst of World War II, a covert German warship vanishes in the Caribbean Sea. Decades later, a Russian warship sinks near the shores of Grand Cayman. Investigative reporter Emerson Moore, after a harrowing incident on Lake Erie's icy expanse, finds solace in the Cayman Islands. There, he becomes entangled with the sinister Jamaican drug kingpin, Pryce Clarke, and his secret operations beneath the waves in Boatswain's Bay near DiveTech. Concurrently, Moore discovers clues about the lost German ship and a perilous scheme by the Soviet Union aimed at the U.S. during the height of the Cuban Missile Crisis.

The story's vibrant characters include Moore's former Navy SEAL comrade Sam Duncan, the iconic island musician Mike "Mad Dog" Adams, a mysterious Jamaican woman, a covert Royal Cayman Police Superintendent, and the colorful patrons of Durty Reid's Bar and Grille in Red Bay.

Spanning from the frosty Lake Erie Islands to the tropical Cayman Islands, The Other Side of Hell is a thrilling narrative filled with treachery, action-packed scuba diving adventures among eels, barracudas, and jellyfish, and a whirlwind of murder and chaos.

#6 Tan Lines

Lake Erie is facing a mysterious crisis as perch populations plummet, raising alarms of bioterrorism or an unknown virus. Amidst this turmoil, the U.S. President vanishes during a joint conference with the Canadian Prime Minister at Ohio State University's Stone Lab on Gibraltar Island. The disappearance occurs just days before a crucial re-nomination convention in Cleveland. Accused of an assassination attempt by the head of the Presidential Protection Detail, investigative reporter Emerson Moore flees, triggering a statewide manhunt. As the search intensifies, it encompasses a missing Secret Service agent and an enigmatic third entity. In a whirlwind of danger including assassination attempts, covert operations, unsolved crimes, and a rogue law enforcement officer, Moore must navigate treacherous waters to exonerate himself and locate the missing President.

#7 Sandustee

Fans of 'National Treasure' and 'The Da Vinci Code' will be captivated by 'Sandustee', a thrilling quest across the globe to uncover a lost biblical artifact, the Nazarene's Code, which grants immense geopolitical power. The narrative weaves a complex tapestry linking historical figures and events, from Osama Bin Laden to Jesus, the twelve disciples, Abraham Lincoln, and the enigmatic Legend of 13, which influences the story's direction with its cryptic significance.

'Sandustee' is a riveting tale brimming with danger, betrayal, underwater adventures, and hints of ancient orders like the Knights Templar and Masonic lore. Investigative reporter Emerson Moore teams up with a striking German scholar in a race against a cunning Russian antagonist to decipher the trail of enigmas.

Their journey spans from the depths of the Red Sea to the vibrant streets of Bodrum, Turkey, and historic locales across Germany, Rhodes, London, Key West, the Dry Tortugas, New Orleans, Washington, D.C., and the quaint towns of Ohio. With each clue they unravel, the shadow of mortality looms ever closer.

#8 Zenobia

In 1991, Emerson Moore lands his first significant investigative role, delving into the Serbian-Croatian conflict in Vukovar. He clashes with a ruthless Serbian commander known as the Vuk. The Vuk, notorious for his crimes against Croatians, also partakes in human trafficking, targeting a young Croatian orphan girl under Moore's protection.

Fast forward to the present, Moore's tranquil life in Put-in-Bay is shattered by a murder and the vanishing of two teenagers, drawing him into the dark realm of trafficking. Undercover in Toledo, he navigates the perilous I-75, delivering victims to a crime lord in Naples. Moore's past haunts him as he encounters a former nemesis, propelling Moore through a tumultuous journey of loss and emotional salvation, surrounded by a vibrant cast of characters.

#9 Missing

Put-in-Bay investigative reporter Emerson Moore finds his world upended after the conviction of mobster Jimmy Diamonds and a daring escape gone awry. Suffering from amnesia, he's led to believe he's Manny Elias, a notorious hitman. After sinister training in Cedar Key, Florida, Moore, as Elias, emerges in Ohio, ensnared in a vendetta against Diamonds' enemies.

Amidst a series of lethal missions, he forms a bond with a woman near his Wooster refuge. The tension culminates in a deadly encounter at a Lake Erie marina, where a fatal twist reveals the truth about Elias. The tale unfolds with relentless pace, showcasing the inner conflict of a man torn between his forgotten morals and the brutal necessities of his assumed role, further complicated when two former comrades become his next targets, leading to a climactic resolution.

#10 Golden Torpedo

Investigative reporter Emerson Moore finds himself entangled in a web of intrigue that ties a submerged WWII U-boat and FDR's demise in 1945 to a terrorist plot. He must unravel the mystery before devastation is unleashed at a vital military base in Florida and a global summit in New Orleans.

In the search for the U-boat, Moore allies with a famed shipwreck hunter and a Turkish marine archaeologist, alongside his captivating daughter and a diverse band of eccentrics, in a perilous quest through the Florida Straits. Stricken by calamity, Moore and a colleague are cast adrift at sea, their survival hanging by a thread.

#11 Chincoteague Calm

Chincoteague Island, a serene location famed for its annual pony swim, is rocked by NASA rocket explosions and a string of mysterious murders. Investigative reporter Emerson Moore finds his tranquil fishing trip on the island cut short as he's drawn into a lethal web of international espionage that threatens NASA's rocket launches. With the aid of Wallops Island's enigmatic NASA director, the caustic head of NASA security, an affable marina owner, and an enigmatic recluse, Moore navigates a labyrinth of potential culprits, ranging from local ruffians to foreign rocketry specialists, all capable of undermining the American space endeavor.

As casualties mount with alarming speed, Moore races against time to unmask the architect of the turmoil and deceit, hoping to thwart the plot against the U.S. space program and save lives, including his own. It's a tale rife with betrayal and shifting allegiances.

#12 Flight

In the tumult of the 1928 Okeechobee Hurricane, a Pinkerton detective aboard a Ford trimotor pursues a treasure-laden train bound for Key West, but both vanish. Investigative reporter Emerson Moore stumbles upon this enigma at Bellevue's train museum in Ohio. While undercover in Key West for a drug trafficking scoop, Moore learns the fate of the missing train.

Survival becomes precarious as Moore dodges assassination, risks exposure by old acquaintances, and embarks on a covert mission to Cuba with the aid of a defense contractor from Cudjoe Key. In Cuba, an alliance forms with a Georgian woman seeking her DEA agent brother, leading to a daring incursion into a drug lord's mountain stronghold. Injured and desperate, Moore's escape through the jungle is a race against death.

#13 Assateague Dark

Investigative reporter Emerson Moore retreats to tranquil Chincoteague Island for solace after a harrowing ordeal in Cuba. However, his respite is short-lived as he's drawn into a perilous drug trafficking scheme on the Delmarva Peninsula. Moore's probe leads to a deadly standoff with a narcotics kingpin at his waterfront stronghold in Cape Charles. Joining forces with the Drug Task Force, Moore embarks on a series of raids, aiming to bring down the elusive kingpin, but as he edges closer, the stakes escalate to a lethal level.

Facing constant danger, Moore relies on his expertise and audacity to stay alive, particularly after a grim twist finds him trapped in a coffin. His fate hangs in the balance: can he outwit death once more? It's a thrilling narrative featuring the iconic Chincoteague Pony Swim, a deadly clash in a Cape Charles eatery, and intense shootouts across various locales, culminating in a tale brimming with relentless thrills and high-octane drama.

#14 Memory Layne (Not an Emerson Moore Adventure)

Zeke Layne's adventures are a captivating blend of humor, heart, and resilience. Zeke, a retired ferry captain living on Lake Erie's shores, navigates the complexities of life with Alzheimer's and a heart condition. His days are filled with the joy of storytelling and the love for his family and animals, including a cherished Chincoteague pony. Despite the challenges posed by his health and the greed of his stepdaughters, Zeke's spirit remains unbroken until disaster strikes. He must rally his dwindling strength in a frantic race to sanctuary.

The novel offers a rich tapestry of characters and experiences that celebrate the power of love and the strength of the human spirit.

#15 Sunset Blues

An enigmatic blast obliterates the waterfront residence of investigative reporter Emerson Moore's Aunt Anne in Put-in-Bay, leaving her whereabouts unknown. Could this be a kidnapping linked to the sinister operations of Russians operating London-style cabs on Lake Erie's South Bass Island and Key West, or a personal attack on Moore?

Moore joins forces with island performer Mike "Mad Dog" Adams, leading them from a fierce confrontation in Detroit with mobster Ruslan Zharkov to Key West, where they assemble a motley crew of distractible eccentrics headed by the notorious Chuck Meier. As the search intensifies, Moore is haunted by the possibility of his aunt's grim fate and stumbles upon an astonishing revelation about the mastermind of her disappearance—a figure bent on revenge against him. Racing against time, Moore faces overwhelming odds to rescue her, battling through emotional turmoil and a dangerous showdown with the devious Zharkov.

#16 White Spider Night

Following the end-of-summer festivities, the tranquil anticipation of autumn was disrupted for the inhabitants of South Bass Island and bustling Put-in-Bay when they learned of the disappearance of a beloved bed & breakfast proprietor. The case of Elke White's vanishing struck the local police as peculiar from the outset, with her spouse, Spider, quickly becoming the focus of the investigation amid whispers of domestic discord and infidelity.

The questions loomed: Was Elke's departure an escape from personal demons, or something more sinister? What drove the act, who was behind it, and how did Middle Bass Island tie into the narrative? A lineup of suspects emerged, akin to aircraft queued for landing. Caught in a web of enigmas, Emerson Moore delves into the case, confronted with a perplexing array of suspects, each piece a fragment of the broader mystery.

#17 Rainbow's End 20th Anniversary Edition

In 1864, Confederate raiders launched a daring mission from Canada to liberate officers held captive on Johnson's Island. The mystery deepens with the discovery of a corpse on Rattlesnake Island, marking the start of a decades-long hunt for an elusive trunk.

Fast forward to 2001, an investigative reporter, while visiting his aunt in Put-in-Bay, tangles with a powerful shipping tycoon as he delves into the raid's history and the trunk's disappearance. Amidst this, he struggles to manage his intense attraction to a married woman he encounters on South Bass Island. The original edition is out of print and is replaced by the rewritten 20th anniversary edition.

#18 Sawdust Joint

Emerson Moore's quest to uncover the mystery behind the deaths of dairy cows and humans leads him on a perilous journey from Jamaica to the French Riviera, and beyond. His investigation intensifies when he infiltrates a suspect British biotech firm.

After a colleague's shocking death, Moore, aided by a tech wizard and an unexpected Canadian ally, confronts a bioterrorist adversary. "Sawdust Joint" escalates into a James Bond-like, adrenaline-fueled escapade, testing Moore's limits amidst casino action, femme fatales, high-speed chases, dangerous cliff climbing, escape from a Moroccan prison and high-stakes showdowns with a formidable foe.

#19 Holden's Promise

Emerson Moore visits Shallotte, North Carolina, seeking a tranquil retreat with a dear friend. However, tranquility eludes him as he's drawn into a web of mystery involving a dubious vessel near Holden Beach's Flounder Pier. The narrative thickens with nocturnal ventures by a former shrimp boat captain on the Shallotte River, his bitter rivalry with a fellow captain, and a series of unsolved crimes, abductions, and maritime mishaps involving teenagers. These elements converge into an enthralling saga.

Meanwhile, the serene community of Holden Beach is jolted by a series of dangerous events stretching from Ocean Isle Beach to a marina in Southport, weaving a tapestry of charming characters and complex relationships.

About the Author
Bob Adamov

Bob Adamov is an award-winning, Ohio mystery adventure author whose stories are based in the Lake Erie South Bass Island resort village of Put-in-Bay, the "Key West of the Midwest." His novels, with the exception of Memory Layne and Alone at Home, follow the adventures of investigative reporter Emerson Moore, and are written in the style of Adamov's favorite author, Clive Cussler.

Adamov was the **featured author at the 2006 Ernest Hemingway Days' Literary Festival** in Key West, voted **2022 Best Lake Erie Author** by Lake Erie Living magazine and **Writer of the Year** by the University of Akron's Wayne College in 2010. Adamov has also presented for several of the **Clive Cussler Collectors' Society conventions.**

A graduate of Kent State University, Adamov resides in Wooster, Ohio. He can often be seen in Put-in-Bay, Key West, Chincoteague, North Carolina's Brunswick Islands and the Cayman Islands with his scuba diving and treasure hunting friends. Previously, he worked for an Arlington, Virginia-based defense contractor in the intelligence sector.

On October 19, 2022, Adamov celebrated the release of his first novel Rainbow's End 20 years earlier with a rewritten 20th anniversary edition. He is working on his 21st novel, Breakwater Bay.